Questions Answered

Questions You Have Always Wished To Ask

OTHER BOOKS AND BOOKLETS BY J.P. VASWANI

In English

10 Commandments of A Successful Marriage
101 Stories For You And Me
108 Pearls of Practical Wisdom
108 Simple Prayers of A Simple Man
108 Thoughts on Success
114 Thoughts on Love
25 Stories For Children and also for Teens
A Little Book of Life
A Treasure of Quotes
Around The Camp Fire
Begin The Day With God
Break The Habit
Burn Anger Before Anger Burns You
Daily Appointment With God
Daily Inspiration
Daily Inspiration (Booklet)
Destination Happiness
Dewdrops of Love
Does God Have Favourites?
Formula For Prosperity
Gateways to Heaven
God In Quest of Man
Good Parenting
Hinduism
How To Embrace Pain
I am a Sindhi
I Luv U, God!
It's All A Matter of Attitude
Joy Peace Pills
Kill Fear Before Fear Kills You
Ladder of Abhyasa
Life After Death
Living Legend
Management Moment By Moment
Many Paths: One Goal
More Snacks For The Soul
Nearer, My God, To Thee!
Peace or Perish
Positive Power of Thanksgiving
Sadhu Vaswani : His Life And Teachings
Saints For You and Me
Saints With A Difference
Secrets of Health And Happiness
Short Sketches of Saints Known & Unknown
Sketches of Saints Known & Unknown
Snacks For The Soul
Swallow Irritation Before Irritation Swallows You
Teachers are Sculptors
The Heart of a Mother
The King of Kings
The Little Book of Freedom From Stress
The Little Book of Prayer
The Little Book of Service
The Little Book of Success
The Little Book of Wisdom
The Little Book of Yoga
The Lord Provides
The Magic of Forgiveness
The One Thing Needful
The Patience of Purna
The Perfect Relationship: Guru and Disciple
The Power of Good Deeds
The Power of Thought
The Seven Commandments of the Bhagavad Gita
The Terror Within
The Way of Abhyasa (How To Meditate)
Thus Have I Been Taught

Thus Spake Sadhu Vaswani
Tips For Teenagers
Trust Me All in All or Not at All
What You Would Like To know About Karma
Whom Do You Love the Most
Why Do Good People Suffer?
You Are Not Alone God Is With You!
You Can Make A Difference

In Hindi:

Dainik Prerna
Dar Se Mukti Paayen
Mrutyu Hai Dwar... Phir Kya?
Santon Ki Leela
Sadhu Vaswani: Unkaa Jeevan Aur Shikshaayen
Safal Vivah Ke Dus Rahasya
Nava Pushp (Bhajans In Hindi and Sindhi)
Prarthna ki Shakti
Laghu Kathayein
Bhakton Ki Uljhanon Kaa Saral Upaai
Bhale Logon Ke Saath Bura Kyon?
Aalwar Santon Ki Mahan Gaathaayen
Atmik Jalpaan
Atmik Poshan
Ishwar Tujhe Pranam
Krodh Ko Jalayen Swayam Ko Nahin
Chahat Hai Mujhe Ik Teri Teri! (Booklet)

In Marathi:

Krodhala Shaanth Kara, Krodhane Ghala Ghalny
Purvee (Burn Anger Before Anger Burns You
Jyanchya Jholit Aahe Prem (Jiski Jholi Mein Hai Py
Yashasvi Vaivahik Jiwanaachi Sutre
(10 Commandments of Successful Marriage
Karma Mhanje Kay? Samjun Ghyaychey
(What Would You Like to Know About Karma
Mrityu Nantarche Jeevan (Life After Death)

In Kannada:

Burn Anger Before Anger Burns You
Life After Death
Why do Good People Suffer
101 Stories For You And Me

In Telugu:

Life after Death
Burn Anger Before Anger Burns You

In Spanish:

Bocaditos Para el Alma (Snacks for the Soul)
Mas Bocaditos Para el Alma (More Snacks for the Soul)
Queme La Ira Antes Que La Ira Lo Queme A Usted(Burn Anger Before Anger Burns You)
Inicia Tu Dia Con Dios (Begin The Day With God)
Sita Diario ku Dios (I Luv U, God!)

In Arabic:

Daily Appointment With God

In Chinese:

Daily Appointment With God

In Dutch:

Begin The Day With God

Questions Answered

Questions You Have Always Wished To Ask

J.P. VASWANI

Compiled and edited by

Prof. Prabha Sampath
and
Krishna Kumari

Gita Publishing House
Pune, (India).
www.dadavaswanisbooks.org

Published by:
Gita Publishing House
Sadhu Vaswani Mission,
10, Sadhu Vaswani Path,
Pune – 411 001, (India).
gph@sadhuvaswani.org

**First to Fifth Editions were published under the title,
"Dada Answers"**
**This Sixth Edition is being published under a new title,
"Questions Answered"**

ISBN: 978-93-80743-01-1

Printed by:
Mehta Offset Pvt. Ltd.
Mehta House,
A-16, Naraina Industrial Area II,
New Delhi – 110 028, (India).
info@mehtaoffset.com

Contents

Compilers' Note

Asatoma satgamaya
Tamasoma jyotirgamaya
Mrityorma amritamgamaya!

Out of unreality, lead me to reality
Out of darkness, lead me to light
Out of death, lead me to Eternity!

Such was the invocation of the ancient *rishis* of India. It was indeed a great ideal that they placed before humankind. But for us, ordinary mortals, the question arises: who is it that will lead us from unreality to reality, from darkness to light, out of ignorance to true knowledge?

The answer is— the Guru, of course!

Questions, questions, questions. They seem to haunt us from the moment we are born till the moment comes when the soul is liberated from the body— and death itself is not the end, for death is indeed the eternal question. Where do we go from here? What becomes of us next? We continue to be overwhelmed by unanswered, unanswerable questions— what, why, where and how.

Indian scholastic tradition has always encouraged the questioning spirit. The disciples of the *ashrams* of ancient India were never expected to take anything they were taught at face value. They were trained to think for themselves, seek clarification, and raise queries before the Guru until they were fully satisfied, and no doubts lingered in their minds.

Dada J.P. Vaswani too, has advocated this questioning spirit among the thousands who have had the privilege of calling themselves his dear disciples and devotees. Dada has always been the pragmatic philosopher who shows rather than tells; one who clarifies, not one who mystifies; one who is ever willing to take us by the hand and lead us on to the Truth we are all seeking. In this, as in his all-giving love, universal compassion and profound wisdom, he belongs to the great tradition of India's seers, sages, seekers and saints. Wherever he travels in the East or the West, he readily turns many of his Public meetings into Question-and-Answer sessions, so that he may lighten the burden that people carry; so that he may dispel the darkness that surrounds them and set their wandering hearts at rest.

Dada's attitude to his interlocutors is refreshingly different— it is not that of the preacher who dogmatizes, nor that of the stern prophet who pontificates. Rather, he is the ideal teacher who elucidates, explains, enlightens and above all, inspires. No question is too abstract, no problem is too difficult for him to dismiss. His understanding of human nature is deep; his readings of the world's great books and scriptures is wide; and his knowledge of the testament of life is profound. No wonder then, that questions placed before him always elicit illuminating deeply satisfying responses.

Dada never evades issues; he does not resort to dogma; he never pronounces judgements. A great seeker of the Truth himself, he pays us the ultimate compliments of treating us as his fellow-pilgrims, fellow-seekers on the path. This attitude makes his responses cordial, positive and brilliantly clear. He does not pronounce precepts from a pedestal; rather, he guides us expertly, carefully, gently to that Truth which actually resides within us— the Truth which we are somehow never able to reach on our own.

This is what makes Dada such a wonderful Guru. He allows us the freedom of spirit to assess, evaluate, question and accept on our own terms. All the time, his guiding, guarding and healing hand leads us unerringly to the Truth we seek.

The questions featured in this book have been addressed to Dada at Public functions, meet-the-press sessions, intimate gatherings and youth get-togethers. Young and old, sceptics and believers and non-believers have felt free to ask Dada about anything under the sun— marital incompatibility and spiritual quest; on the future of humanity and the nature of friendship; on love and hatred; on war and peace; on animal rights and astrology— no subject is taboo; no question is dismissed without a carefully considered answer.

Wisdom shared is wisdom multiplied. The compilers of this book take great pleasure in offering this memorable collection to the reading public, for it enables them to share the blessings of Dada's guidance with genuine seekers all over the world. Readers will find that the questions featured here are the very ones which have risen in their minds and hearts at one time or another. It is hoped that they will find enlightenment, inspiration, and guidance from this book, as thousands of devotees have found in Question-and-Answer sessions with Dada held all over the world.

Prabha Sampath
Krishna Kumari

Anger

Anger is the foundation of every evil.
– Muhammad Husan Askari

We boil at different degrees.
– Ralph Waldo Emerson

The fire you kindle for your enemy often
burns yourself more than him.
– Chinese Proverb

1

Why do people get angry?

The simple cause of anger, I believe, is self-will. Whenever I want a thing to be done in a particular way and it is done in a different way, I get angry. If only I can curb my self-will by surrendering it to the Will divine, I will not be angry. Once I realise that everything that happens, happens according to the Will of God and in the Will of God is my highest good, I shall never, never, get angry.

I read about a scientist who worked at the turn of the last century on barometric pressures. For twenty long, painstaking years, he noted down his readings. After twenty years of strenuous labour he wanted to collate the readings and formulate a theory. Just about that time, his maid-servant applied for leave to attend the marriage of her cousin. She left a substitute behind.

The very first evening, as the professor returned from his usual walk, he found all his papers missing. He called the substitute and asked, "Where are my papers?"

"Sir, as I was cleaning your table, I found a heap of papers, dirty and soiled. I flung them into the fire, and have kept clean sheets of paper instead," she quietly explained.

The professor had every reason to get mad at her. But do you know what he did? He said to himself, "This has happened according to the Will of God. There must be some good in it. Thy Will be done, O Lord!"

If only we realised that whatever happens, happens according to the divine Will, we would never succumb to anger.

Can anger be justified? The anger of the mother on her child, or of the teacher on the pupil— can it be righteous?

Yes, anger can be righteous. Anger becomes righteous when it is the duty of the person to get angry. When a person feels it is his duty to get angry, he dissociates himself from his self-will. He himself becomes a spectator to his own anger. The historical example of righteous anger is given us in the New Testament. Jesus visits a temple and finds the priests desecrating it. He gets righteously angry and says to the priests, "What is it that you are doing? You have converted my Father's home into a commercial house."

This type of anger— righteous anger— will not degrade a man but will ennoble him.

Dada, can you elaborate more on this righteous anger?

Anger is a two-edged sword. There is a type of anger which drains energy and produces tension. There is another type that is a positive and a creative life force— and this is known as righteous anger. When it is my duty to be angry, and I become angry— that is righteous anger. A parent sometimes has to be angry with a child for the good of the child. A teacher sometimes has to be angry with a student for the good of the student. An employer sometimes has to be angry with an employee for the good of the organisation.

If you find a man molesting a woman, or ill treating an animal on the road side, you have every right to be angry. Anger becomes righteous when you get angry to defend the rights of another, without any selfish motive.

Is it true that anger begets anger?

In anger, I believe, there is a chain reaction. If a person gets angry with another and the person who receives the anger is not able to react immediately, he stores up that anger and throws it on someone else. There is a chain reaction, as it were. Anger keeps on passing from one person to another.

There was a Russian couple who loved each other beyond words. Everyday to them was as though it was the first day of their marriage. Every evening, the wife would await the coming of her husband from the office. As he approached the compound, she would go out and open the gate of the compound, sit with him in the car and drive with him upto the garage.

One day, this man returned from his office in an awful mood. He had probably been scolded by his superior. His blood was boiling. When his wife came to greet him at the compound gate, he locked the door of his car and didn't allow her to get in. She was naturally worried.

When he got down from the car, she lovingly said to him, "What is the problem?"

"You keep talking all the time," he said to her impatiently. "I don't want to hear your dirty voice ever again," he angrily retorted.

The wife was taken aback. The lotus of her heart drooped. Those words went so deep into her heart that never again for the rest of her life, did she speak a single word to her husband. Even after forty years, when the husband was on his death bed and pleaded with her to utter just a single word, she still could not do so. Therefore, we must learn to control anger in all situations.

Can humour help us?

Mahatma Gandhi, the father of the nation, had these words inscribed on one of the walls of the small cottage in which he lived at *Sevagram*: "If you are in the right, you don't need to lose your temper. If you are in the wrong, you cannot afford to lose it."

Yes, a rich sense of humour is very useful to control one's anger.

Professor Blackie put up a notice outside a classroom, "Professor Blackie will take classes tomorrow." A mischievous boy happened to pass by. He read the notice and rubbed the 'c' out of the 'classes.' The notice read, "Professor Blackie will take lasses tomorrow."

Professor Blackie happened to pass by. Responding to the student's mischief, instead of getting angry he rubbed the 'l' out of the 'lasses' and now the notice read, "Professor Blackie will take 'asses' tomorrow." The joke was turned on the students.

Can you recommend some spiritual ways of controlling anger? Does meditation help?

Meditation helps greatly in controlling anger because one of the purposes of meditation is to raise the frequency of vibrations. And when the frequency of our vibrations is raised, we arrive at a point where anger can come nowhere near us.

It is because we are moving on a lower level of consciousness that trivial things irritate us. At the higher level nothing disturbs us. And it is the primary purpose of meditation to lift up our consciousness from the lower *chakras* to the higher ones.

Of Alexander the great, it is said, that when he visited India, he wanted to take back with himself a *yogi* to Greece.

Finding a *yogi*, Alexander said to him, "Come with me, for my people are eager to meet a *yogi*."

The *yogi* showed a lack of interest at which the great world conqueror flew into an uncontrollable rage.

It was the first time that his request had been turned down. Unsheathing his sword, he said to the *yogi*, "Do you know I can cut you into pieces? I am Alexander, the world conqueror!"

Quietly the *yogi* answered, "You call yourself a world conqueror, but you are only a slave of my slave."

"How is that?" asked Alexander, perplexed.

The *yogi* replied, "Anger is my slave. And you have become a slave to anger."

Could you suggest what one should do when one gets angry?

If possible, one should turn the face of anger towards oneself instead of getting angry at others. The faults I see in others are merely reflections of my own faults. Therefore, it is better to turn my anger on myself.

One way of controlling anger is to allow some time to pass. Before giving vent to our anger, let us tell ourselves, "I shall get angry, but only after I have counted upto 100."And you will find that your anger will have already subsided by then.

Yet another helpful suggestion is, drink a glass of water just when you find yourself getting angry and the intensity of your anger will get considerably reduced.

The daily habit of sitting in silence will also go a long way in strengthening your defences against anger. A very helpful way to control anger is to write a letter to the one who has angered you and pour into it all the anger of your heart. Then tear the letter and throw it into the dustbin.

To Mahatma Gandhi, there came a man who had been ill-treated by a friend. And Gandhi said to him, "Why don't you write a very strong letter to him, pouring into it all the anger that you carry in your heart?" The man did as he was told and, bringing the letter to Gandhi said to him, "May I post the letter to him?"

"No", said Mahatma Gandhi, "now that you feel relieved, throw it into the waste paper basket!"

What is the difference between suppression and control of anger?

There are three ways of handling anger. There is the way of expression, which so many of us follow. We feel angry and we show it in our words and actions.

The second is the way of suppression. We suppress anger because we don't like to show people that we are angry. As psychologists tell you, this creates complexes.

Then, there is the third, and the right way of handling anger. That is the way of forgiveness. If we forgive, then we rise above anger.

Can anger affect the health of the individual?

When a person gets angry, he activates certain glands in the body. This leads to an outpouring of adrenaline and other stress hormones, with noticeable physical consequences. The face reddens, blood pressure increases, the voice rises to a higher pitch, breathing becomes faster and deeper, the heart-beats become harder, the muscles of the arms and legs tighten. The body moves into an excited state.

If a man is given to anger, all these processes are repeated again and again and he will land himself into serious health problems. The cumulative effect of the hormones released during anger episodes can add to the risk of coronary and other life-threatening diseases including strokes, ulcers and high blood pressure. It is, therefore, in your own interest that you learn to control— or in any case, reduce— your anger.

Recent researches have proved that people who are often prone to anger get heart attacks more easily than others. It has also been proved that when a person is calm, peaceful, happy, the digestive processes work normally. When man comes under the influence of anger, the digestive processes are paralysed. Therefore, doctors recommend that you should be cheerful and in good humour when you eat. If you don't feel cheerful, it is better that you do not eat. Stomach ulcers are caused by anger. They recur even after operations, if the resentment continues.

Anger affects the entire body, for anger is poison. I read about a mother who was given to frequent bouts of anger. Her infant received milk from her while she was in an angry mood. Soon the baby died. Anger throws poison into the blood stream.

How can we handle anger constructively?

There are three ways of handling anger. There is, firstly, the way of expression. Psychiatrists tell us that it is good to express anger. Expression gives you relief, for you get some satisfaction at having given a piece of your mind to the other person. This relief, however is temporary. Resentments build up again, and you are ready for another spill out. Gradually, anger becomes a habit and the time comes when you become a slave to anger. You are controlled by anger: and anger is a terrible master. I read about a mother who, in a mood of anger, threw her own child into the fire!

The second is the way of suppression. It is not the right way. Suppression drives anger into the subconscious, where it works its havoc.

The third way is the right way. It is the way of forgiveness, of patience and forbearance. Forgive, and be free! Every night, before you retire, go over the happenings of the day. Has someone cheated you? Has someone offended you? Has someone hurt or ill-treated you? Has someone spread scandals against you? Call out that person's name and say, "Mr. X, I forgive you!" "Mrs. Y, I forgive you!" "Miss Z, I forgive you!" You will have a peaceful sleep and beautiful dreams. The right way to overcome anger is the way of forgiveness.

Dada, can you give us some practical suggestions to overcome anger?

1. The best and surest way of controlling anger is the way of self-realisation. Once you realise who you are, you will never be angry. This implies identification with our highest self.

2. Develop the will to control anger. Realise the uselessness of anger. We may not harm the person with whom we feel angry but we surely harm ourselves when we are angry.

3. Accept every incident and accident as God's Will. Rejoice in whatever His Will brings to you. You will then arrive at a stage where nothing will upset you and make you angry.

4. Seek the help of God to control your anger. Without His grace, you can achieve nothing.

5. Avoid occasions for anger. Whenever you find yourself in a situation which makes you angry, turn away from it.

6. Avoid haste— for haste is the mother of anger, even as hatred is its father.

7. Whenever you feel anger approaching, keep your mouth shut and your lips sealed. When you speak, speak lovingly, softly, gently.

8. If you are unable to keep quiet, hum to yourself a simple tune. This will help you to relax and remain calm.

9. When angry, drink a glass or two of cold water, or go out and take a brisk walk, or run or jog. Exercise will burn up your negative emotional energy.

10. Count upto ten, or if you are very angry, count upto hundred.

Astrology

I am the master of my fate: I am the captain of my soul.
— W. E. Henley

The Moving Finger writes; and, having writ, moves on: Nor all thy piety nor wit shall lure it back to cancel half a Line nor all thy Tears wash out a Word of it.
— Edward Fitzgerald, Rubaiyat of Khayyam

Dadaji, should I believe in astrology, horoscopes, birth-charts and spirits?

If I say, you must not believe in them, you will not listen to me. Supposing right now a palmist came here and started reading your palms free of charge, so many of you will quietly leave this hall and go and have your palms read. So, if I tell you don't do it, you will not listen, but let me tell you, there is some truth in astrology. There is truth in birth-charts. There is truth in horoscopes, but we need the right type of people who know how to read them.

There was a time when we had real astrologers. Today, even if you get an astrologer who is able to read horoscopes properly, you are not sure if your horoscope was cast properly.

Usually when a person passes through a period of suffering, he goes to the astrologer and asks, "How long do I have to suffer?" But remember, suffering is a gift of God. It is only in periods of suffering that you enrich your interior life. It is only in periods of suffering that you develop your moral and spiritual muscles. Therefore, whenever suffering comes, greet it and say to it, "you have come to me out of the hands of the Lord. I accept you as His *prasadam*." Then suffering will lose its sting and will leave you with the lesson it has come to teach you.

If the stars of the husband are bad, they say, that the wife should put water and milk on the peepal tree. What connection do the stars have with the peepal tree?

It is a matter of faith. The two have no connection. The stars have no connection whatsoever with giving milk and water to the *peepal* tree. But it is a matter of faith. If you do it with faith, then you generate power. That power may not affect your husband's stars but will affect you. And you will begin to accept whatever the stars hold for your husband with greater patience and deeper wisdom.

Conversion

I went to America to convert the Indians: but oh, who shall convert me?
— *John Wesley*

If you asked me which form of God you should meditate upon, I should say: fix your attention on that form which appeals to you most; but know for certain that all forms are the forms of one God alone. He is blessed indeed who has known all as one.
— *Sri Ramakrishna Paramahansa*

Like the bee, gathering honey from different flowers, the wise man accepts the essence of different Scriptures and sees only the good in all religions.
— *Srimad Bhagavatam*

13

Dada, what are your views on conversion?

True conversion is not a change of label. Merely making a Hindu a Christian or vice versa is not conversion. By conversion, Jesus meant not change of label or conformity to a creed or a dogma, but change of mind and heart. The emphasis in the teaching of Jesus is on life, not words.

True conversion is a change of mind, a change of attitude, which results in the transformation of the individual. His life itself becomes new. It is as though the man is reborn, has taken a second birth. Man is born of the flesh. He needs to be reborn of the Spirit.

Should we leave our religion and choose another?

No one ever thinks of leaving his family. Even so, we must never think of discarding our religion. Significant are the words of the Lord in the *Gita*, "One's own *dharma*, even if imperfect, is better than the *dharma* of another, well discharged. Better death in one's *dharma*: the *dharma* of another is full of fear."

Lokamanya Tilak's words are worth meditating upon, "Death in one's *dharma* brings new birth: success in an alien path means only successful suicide."

In any case, before you decide to get converted to another religion (and this is like giving up your mother), you must first be acquainted with your own. Hinduism is a great religion. To it tributes have been paid by some of the greatest minds of humanity. And in the deepening darkness of these days, many have declared that the light will once again travel from the East, from the teachings of the great *rishis* and saints of India.

Why doesn't Hinduism permit conversion?

The main note of Hinduism is one of respect and goodwill for other creeds. In a sense, Hinduism may be regarded as the first example in the world of a missionary religion. Only its missionary spirit is different from that associated with the proselytizing creeds. It did not regard it as its mission to convert humanity to any one opinion. Hinduism has the large comprehensive unity of a living organism with a fixed orientation.

The Hindus never went out to conquer or convert. They have been worshippers of truth and ultimate victory belongs to the truth.

Hinduism has been rightly regarded as the mother of all religions. It has truly been the mother of all religions. Therefore all religions have thrived in India. No religion has ever been persecuted in India. Christianity was welcomed, Zoroastrianism was welcomed, Judaism was welcomed and so was Islam.

Why should a Christian want to convert a Hindu to Christianity and vice versa?

What matters is the way a man lives: the way he worships in a temple or a church is not very important. Attachment to a particular form of worship may even become an obstacle in the way of his spiritual progress. And insistence on a creed may in some cases, become the cause of violent quarrels leading to bloodshed and eventually, utter disbelief in God Himself.

I recall what an American Christian brother said to me in New York, "Why do our missionaries go to the trouble of visiting distant lands and converting the people to Christianity? Why can't they convert the Christians in America to Christianity? If the Christians in America accept the teaching of Christ, what a wonderful country America would be!"

In Sind, there was a holy man of Islam, Sachal was his name. And to Sachal there came, one day, a *mullah* (Muslim priest), saying, "Tomorrow we are converting a Hindu to Islam. We want you to be present on the occasion and give us your blessings."

Quietly answered this holy man, "When you convert a Muslim to Islam (i.e.make him a true Muslim), call me, and I shall gladly be present on the occasion."

DADA on himself

What am I?
A tiny candle:
The flame is Thine!

What am I?
An earthen lamp:
The light is Thine!

Dada, can you please tell us, who are you?

I am a seeker and a student. I seek to be a servant of humanity. I love to think of the whole world as my country and to do good as my religion. I aspire to tread the path of humility and love. Love everyone, not only those who are 'good' but those whom the world regards as 'evil'. Love not only men but also all creatures who breathe the breath of life.

What is your religion?

God gave me birth in a Hindu family. I love to think of the Hindu faith as *Sanatana Dharma*— the Eternal Religion. I believe that all religions are true. They are so many paths to the One Reality. Differences and discord in the name of religion are meaningless. I love to think of myself as a member of the Church Universal which brings together people belonging to different faiths who will join hands in the one constructive, the one creative task of building a kingdom of God on earth.

Dada, can you tell us of one of the earliest lessons life has taught you?

One of the earliest lessons I learnt was when I was a school student. I realised that time was the most precious of all possessions. Time is our capital. Every minute— every moment— is precious. There is a Chinese proverb which says, "An inch of time is an inch of gold. But an inch of gold cannot buy an inch of time." We realise the value of the moment only when the last moment arrives.

Alexander, the greatest conqueror the world has known, was defeated by a tiny insect. He died of malarial fever from a mosquito bite. As he lay dying in his tent, he asked, "Is there anyone who will give me a healthy breath of his life? In exchange I will give him my whole empire!" There was no answer.

It was then that Alexander exclaimed, "I wasted millions upon millions of my breaths in carving out an empire in exchange for which I cannot get even a single breath!"

The river of time flows on. The hours quickly change into days, the days into months and the months into years. Suddenly, one day, the bell rings and the call goes forth, "Vacate the house (of the body)!" The body drops down and man realises that he has lost the golden opportunity of the human birth. We must be very careful about our time. We must use it creatively and never forget that every moment is just the right time to do the right thing.

If we wait for more opportune moments, we might have to wait till eternity.

Dada, there is always a million dollar smile on your face. What is the secret?

The secret is a simple one. I seek to live as a little child who knows that its mother is near and it has naught to fear. No mother would wish to bring her child to any harm. And so, in everything that happens— in every incident and accident, every illness and adversity— there is a meaning of the divine Mother's mercy. She is all love and all wisdom. She is too loving to punish, too wise to make a mistake. And so nothing can ever go wrong. All is well, as all was well and will ever be well, both tomorrow and a hundred years hence.

The person, who believes in this, will always continue to smile the smile of bliss. The secret of the carefree life is— to walk with God today, and trust Him for the morrow!

Of course, it is the divine Mother's grace that holds me. I shall continue to smile only as long as Her grace holds me, upholds me. If She were to withdraw Her grace even for a moment, I would crash and be broken into bits.

Sadhu Vaswani always had a radiant smile on his lips. When they asked him the reason, he said, "I have a friend. He protects me. He guards me in illness. He blesses me everyday. And He stretches forth His arms of love to enfold me in the silence and darkness of the night. He is your friend too. Indeed, He is the Friend of friends!"

Sadhu Vaswani's smile was the smile of one who felt the joy of God's presence all the time. It is a joy, which is open to each one of us. Each one of us can become a smile millionaire.

Which is your most memorable day?

Everyday that I spent with my master, everyday that I continue to spend with my master is a memorable day. Every moment that I am at his lotus feet is, indeed, memorable!

You have travelled all over the world. Which spot on this earth is your most favourite spot?

I have not even travelled all over Pune. I have not even seen the entire Main Street. To tell you honestly, I have not even seen the entire Mira Hall. But this question, I am asked at many places. And my answer is, "This, here, where I am at the moment!" Because my most favourite spot is where my beloved master keeps me. When he keeps me in Pune, Pune is my favourite spot. Wherever in the world he keeps me, that is my favourite spot.

Which are your favourite lines, quotes from any spiritual book?

I usually wake up with some quotation, some lines from a scripture and I keep on repeating them throughout the day. It keeps me in a state of recollection. I would advise every aspirant on the spiritual path to do that.

The mind keeps on wandering. The wandering of the mind is terrible. In a minute it wanders so much. To keep it focused, the one thing that may be helpful, is to pick up a good thought, a God-thought, any thought that appeals to the mood of the day. Keep on repeating it— meditate on it for a few minutes and, during the day, save a few seconds, preferably after every hour and repeat the thought to yourself, again and again. You will see that the entire day is spent well.

If society were to offer you a gift for your birthday, what would you ask for?

More opportunities of service.

You are a science graduate. Your thesis for a doctorate was indeed favourably assessed by the renowned scientist, Dr C. V. Raman, but at that stage you waived a doctorate and turned to spirituality. You must really have a more thorough and unified perspective. Usually we categorise anybody with a spiritual bent as someone who has lost contact with the realities of the world and science.

Do you know what the word for spirituality is in Sanskrit? It is *atmavidya*, which means, science of the Spirit. So right from the very ancient times in India, there has been a scientific approach to matters of the Spirit.

What is your philosophy?

My philosophy is simple. It is the philosophy of acceptance. Accept everything that comes to you as a gift from God. There is a meaning of mercy in everything that happens. God is all love. God is all wisdom. Experiences come to us as calamities, illnesses, adversities, and in other forms. But behind them all is the Divine Hand at work. There is a meaning of mercy in everything that happens. Therefore accept, rejoice and move forward.

Who is your favourite disciple?

I have a very favourite disciple. I cannot live without him. For me to live without that favourite disciple would amount to death. That favourite disciple is myself. My disciple and I live together. I tell him many things. I tell him we have to learn many things.

What is your concept of time?

Mahatma Gandhi said that if you have to be truthful, you have to be punctual. If you are a devotee of truth, then you must be very punctual and stick to time. If I am five minutes late then I have not only wasted my five minutes, but five minutes of many people.

What are your beliefs?

Basically, I believe in fellowship with all creation. The creation of God is bound by golden chains to the feet of the one God— the one divine Father of all. At His Lotus Feet, we are all one— men of different religions and no religion. No one is an alien in the Kingdom of God. All sectarian strife, and quarrels in the name of religion, are due to lack of understanding. I belong to no sect. My faith is to worship the one mystery and to do good to all.

Is there anything that you are afraid of?

I am afraid of losing the pleasure of my guru, my Lord. That I may ever displease him, is my greatest fear.

Dada, is your outlook secular?

Yes, my vision of life is secularistic in the spiritual sense and not in the religious sense. The spirit of humanity is one. In this life, we have to work for the unity of mankind. The coming civilisation will be built on a nobler thought, and that thought is, "You are me, I am you." In that oneness, joy, peace and love will grow.

How do you keep so young at 82?

Proximity with my Mother, the *Jagat Janani* of the universe who looks after me like a child, doesn't allow me to grow up. I am just a child in Her lap. With all the love that She showers on me, I feel like a five-year old. I am a five-year old!

Youth is not a matter of age, it is a condition and a state of mind. When one is receptive and prepared to learn, it does not matter what age he is. Always be prepared to perform new experiments in the laboratory of life. A person can be old at the age of 18 and young at 81.

Does anything worry you?

I do not let anything worry me. Why should I? Everything that happens is in accordance with the divine plan of my Mother. How can She permit anything to happen which may hurt or harm me?

It is true, I have to face problems, again and again. But I have faith that everything that comes to me is *prasadam* out of the holy hands of the Mother. It may be bitter, it may be sweet.

What is the first thing you do each day?

I spend some time alone, in silence. I speak to God, pray, meditate, get my doubts cleared from Him before the rigmarole of the day begins.

Do you plan your day?

Sadhu Vaswani used to say, "Plan nothing, win everything."

Ultimately everything is planned by God in a manner that will eventually be beneficial to you. But, yes, we do need to plan our lives. However, do not set plans into steel frames. I take things the way they are served to me. Remember one thing, "God upsets our plans to set up His own." And His plans are perfect. There is a meaning in everything He does.

What is the one thing you cannot do without?

God. I will do without breath but not without God, I will do without food but not without God.

Dada, have you seen God?

I see God when I see Him in you all. Not merely in all human beings but also in all creatures that breathe the breath of life. Indeed, in everything that is around me.

True *darshan* is when I see the one Light in all. That is the great message that India has to give. *Darshan* of God is not seeing a picture of God on the wall. True *darshan* is seeing the Beloved in every one.

If you had an opportunity to make a new world, how would you make it?

I would not meddle with God's plan. It is a perfect plan and can leave no room for improvement.

Death

Death never takes the wise man by surprise; he is always ready to go.
— Jean de La Fontaine

Every man knows he must die, but no one believes it.
— Yiddish Proverb

When we die, we leave behind us all we have, and take with us all we are.
— Anonymous

Death is not a period but a comma in the story of life.
— Dr. Amos J. Tarver

Death is like sunset, which is only an appearance. For what is sunset here is sunrise elsewhere. In reality, the sun never sets. Likewise, there is no death. Death is only an illusion, an appearance. For death here is birth elsewhere.
— Sadhu Vaswani

Liberation Li... sion. Egoism. Violent Dre... Spiritual... Woman Yoga... Bhagavad Gita & Worry. Science ... Seeker Service Silence Spiritual... Woman Yoga Bhagavad Gita & Frustration, Worry. Science ... Vibrations Willpower Of The World. Bhagavad Gita & Rituals Sadhu Vaswani Science ... Selfishness, Frustration, Thought Power Understanding Rituals Sadhu Vaswani Education Faith Fe... Meditati...

Dada, do you believe in death?

If you ask me what I believe in then let me tell you that I don't believe that there is any death. Humanity suffers from illusions. One of the greatest illusions is death.

What is death? Let me give you an incident from the life of Sri Ramakrishna Parmahansa. He passed away on the night of the 15th of August, 1883, at the age of fifty. His wife, Sharadamani, who is regarded as the holy mother, felt that she had become a widow and had no right to wear bangles on her arms. In those days, widows were not supposed to wear bangles on their arms. She had worn those bangles when she had got married at the age of five to Sri Ramakrishna who was twenty three at that time. In the meantime, her wrists had grown. She could not take off the bangles. She applied soap and many other things, but the bangles would not slip out. She said, "I have no other choice, let me break these bangles." She took a hammer in her hand to break them. She was about to strike when she heard a voice. It was the voice of Ramakrishna, and the voice said, "Sharda, what are you doing? I have not died. I have but passed from one room to another."

That is what death is. Death is only a movement from one room to another. It is very much like sunset. The sun appears to set, but you know that the sun never sets. What is sunset here, is sunrise elsewhere. What is death here, is birth elsewhere.

We asked Sadhu Vaswani, what is death? And he said, "death is a bridge between this world and the next. The next world is a better, nobler, happier, more beautiful, more radiant and happier world than this world." We do not really need to have any fear of death.

How can we overcome fear of death?

Sing the Name of God. Sing it as often as you can. Sing it with every breath that you take in or send out. And as you sing the Name, breathe out the aspiration, "The sea is vast: my skiff is small. But Thy Name, I know will take me across!" As you sing the Name in love and in faith, all fear of death will vanish from your heart as mist before the rising sun. You will then learn to look upon death as a bridge between you and your beloved. And you will long for the day when you may be called upon to cross the bridge. And you will exclaim in the words of St. Francis, "Welcome, sister death!" Death then, will lose its sting. Death will become a door entering which you may behold the beauteous face of the Beloved and abide in His presence for ever and ever more!

What is the way that can lead us to deliverance from death?

We must take note of three truths:

1.   Know! That transient are all earthly things and forms. All that you see around you will, one day, perish. Everything carries within it the seed of decay. The potter makes earthen vessels: they all must break, one day. Such is the life of man. A man lives a hundred years or longer, yet must he, one day, depart. The rich and the poor, the young and the old, the wise and the unwise— are subject to death.

2.   This, too, know! That there is no escaping death. When the hour arrives, not all the armies of kings and conquerors can save you from death. So it is that while friends and relatives helplessly look on and shed tears, their dearly-loved ones are snatched away by death— like animals that are led to the slaughter house.

3.   Knowing this, the wise do not grieve over the dead. Grief and lamentation do not bring the dead to life. Rather they add to our suffering and rob us of our richest treasure— peace of mind. The wise ones aspire to peace. They grieve not, nor do they lament. They walk the way of acceptance. They accept whatever

comes—discomfort, disease, death—and so overcome suffering and sorrow. And having overcome sorrow they are from sorrow freed, and they enter into the peace that defies description. They are the truly blessed ones.

Will I meet my dear ones after death?

To this question, the answer is yes.

Normally, we meet our near and dear ones, after death. For the period that elapses between the death of one physical body and the taking on of another physical body—the period between what is called death and rebirth— covers many, many years, according to the earth calendar.

Suppose someone has put off his physical body today. A long time will elapse before he comes back to the earth-plane, wearing another physical body. The journey after death, the journey through the astral region— through the purgatory and the heaven world and the realm that lies beyond and back to the earth, takes a sufficiently long period. During this period we, who are living on earth today, will have dropped our physical bodies and moved on to the astral world, where we shall meet our near and dear ones.

What should be our attitude towards the dead?

To this question my answer is though we are unable to see those whom we call dead, though we are unable to hear them, they can nonetheless see us and hear us. They cannot hear our words, but they can hear our thoughts. For they, whom we call dead, are minds without bodies, and their minds can read our minds. They hear our thoughts. Therefore, we should be careful about our thoughts in regard to the dead. We should try to overcome our grief and send out to them thoughts of love and goodwill. We should pray for them and wish them well in their journey. Our attitude towards the dead should be that of a mother or a wife whose son or husband has gone overseas to seek his fortune. Surely, the mother or wife of such a person would send him encouraging messages from time to time, words of love and goodwill and cheer. If, instead, the wife writes him letters containing tales of woe and grief, the condition of the husband would be miserable. He cannot come back to his wife to console her. And thinking of the sorrows of his wife, whom he loves, he feels unhappy.

Can astrology predict the exact time of death?

To this my answer is, the stars indicate: they do not compel. Astrology can only tell you the time when death is likely to occur. You must not forget that, that which is threatened does not necessarily befall. Further, astrology is not like arithmetic. A sum in arithmetic can have only one answer. In astrology, so many factors are involved that it is quite likely that the astrologer, whom you have consulted, has not considered all these factors, with the result that his calculations may be far from correct. Astrology is more of an art than a science and much depends upon the astrologer who prepared your horoscope and the one who reads it.

Let me say, however, that in every horoscope there are periods when death is likely to occur. And if you are forewarned, you can be very careful and so can avoid death. I have known cases in which the faith and will power of the person concerned, or someone close to him have helped the person to tide over the crisis. Once the period is crossed over, conditions become normal, until another such period enters your life.

What is the age at which man should wish to die?

There are some who believe with the great French writer, Anatole France, that man should die in the prime of his youth. Anatole France taught that man should live like a butterfly and, drinking beauty, quickly die. I believe otherwise.

The teaching has been given to us that man should attain to maturity before he leaves the physical body. The physical body is not had without great labour. In each incarnation, we have to undergo periods of infancy, childhood, and youth, before we can attain full maturity of our faculties. Therefore, we must not wish to die at an early age, but aspire to attain at least the biblical age of three score years and ten.

It is only when the body becomes old or diseased or otherwise uninhabitable, that we should wish for the release which death brings to the soul. Until such time, we should continue to use the body as an instrument for our spiritual evolution. Therefore, we should strive to keep the body pure and clean and strong and, with every breath of our being, praise the Lord and sing His holy Name, and dedicate the body to the service of God and His suffering children.

What is the best way to die?

There are two types of death. There is a peaceful or natural way of dying: and there is the unpeaceful or unnatural way of dying. The best way to die is in a natural way. This occurs in a variety of ways.

As the years roll on, and a man grows older, his arteries, i.e. the blood vessels, become more and more inelastic and the heart finds it increasingly difficult to pump the blood through the inelastic channels of the arteries. The circulation of the blood suffers in consequence and the different organs of the body do not receive an adequate supply of blood which is necessary for their proper functioning. Thus one organ of the body or another gets out of order, depriving the system of some essential product or service, which ultimately results in the death of the body. This is a natural form of death.

But the best form of death is that in which a man dies with his mind fixed on the Lord, his heart filled with holy love, and his lips uttering the Name divine!

What of those who die suddenly, say, in an accident?

In the case of a man who dies in an accident, the soul, as it were, is suddenly pushed out of the body. Because death has come so quickly, it is dazed. For some time, the soul may not even realise that it has been separated from the physical body. In the astral world, there are a number of service groups. Some are charged with the task of attending to such souls who are suddenly ejected from their physical bodies. These watchers hover like hawks in the astral world, watching for incoming souls who are in need of help. Immediately they rush to their aid and help them to adjust to new conditions.

In several cases, those that die in accidents soon reincarnate to complete the work of their earlier incarnation. But if a person who dies in an accident has lived a reasonably good, pure life, devoted to the service of his fellow beings, such a soul need not reincarnate immediately. Such a soul goes at once into a state of quiet, harmonious sleep, out of which he awakens in the higher astral or heaven world, the vibrations of which are in tune with his own.

In certain cases, a man does not die immediately after the accident, but enters into a state of coma, which may last for many days, before he finally quits the body. In such cases, the outgoing soul can be greatly helped by offering prayers for him at his bedside, if possible, and by reading from scriptures of the faith to which he belongs. Even when he is in deep unconsciousness the dying person can hear what is being recited. This is of great help and should be kept up until he breathes his last.

What of those who are sent to the gallows or who die of electrocution?

Such persons are ejected, against their will, from the physical world. They do not want to die but are forcibly dragged to the death chamber. In their last moments, their hearts are filled with hatred and,

and not unoften, with a violent thirst for revenge. When a man dies in this condition, he becomes a wandering spirit, or what we commonly call, a ghost. Many of you may laugh at the mention of the word, ghost. But believe me, there are ghosts— wandering spirits. They gravitate naturally to vicious atmospheres, to places of sin and vice. There they look out for some weak willed persons and fasten themselves upon them. Cases of psychic possession are too many to be ignored. Therefore, I ask especially young men and women not to visit places of vice, for in doing so, they invite this kind of possession.

There are some innocent persons who, due to an error of judgement or otherwise, are condemned to capital punishment. There are others— patriots of the purest ray serene— who, for no fault of theirs are condemned to die on the gallows, by a cruel, despotic government. Such persons, in the moment of death, should have no thought of vengeance in their hearts, no feeling of resentment or hatred. In the moment of death, let their hearts be filled with the noblest and highest aspirations of which they are capable. If there is someone they love, let them think of him, so that in the moment of death, their hearts are filled with pure and holy love. Let them feel that love, in the greatest, purest possible measure. When a person dies with feelings of love in his heart, whatever be the mode of his death, he straightaway enters into deep and peaceful sleep, out of which he awakens in the higher section of the astral world.

What of those who commit suicide?

The person who commits suicide becomes, immediately after death, an earthbound spirit. He feels more unhappy and restless after suicide than when he was in the physical body. He discovers, too late, that he is not merely a physical body whose consciousness will disappear like a candle light when the flame is extinguished. He finds that he cannot die. The misery, the sorrow, the anguish from which he thought he could escape by committing suicide, have been aggravated. His agony has increased.

The man who commits suicide finds that, instead of solving his problems, the suicide has only intensified its worst features. He feels that it would have been far better if, instead of committing suicide, he had slept over it and considered the situation the next morning or sought the help and advice of a spiritual elder, or prayed to the Lord for guidance. Life is given us by God. It is only He who can take it away. If we take the law in our own hands, we have to pay a heavy price for it.

Can we do anything to help the man who has committed suicide?

Yes, we can do much to help the person who has committed suicide and is now become an earthbound spirit. He continues to be within an orbit where our help can reach him from this side. Love is the great creative power, at every level of life. If there is someone who loves the person who has committed suicide, he can render him help by surrounding the unfortunate one with the healing thoughts of sympathy and love. The help of healing angels can also be invoked through prayer. Through the power of meditation, the rays of love divine can be sent to the unfortunate one so that they surround him and give rest to his restless soul, and wake up within him his own spiritual powers which alone can free him from his self imposed shackles.

Could you tell us how many souls there are? Is there only one soul or are there as many souls as there are humans?

The sun is one. The sun shining in the sky is one, but if you keep one million pots of water here, you will have one million reflections of the sun. Similarly, there is one universal soul, but its reflections are many.

Discipline

Do your work the same in success and misfortune. This evenness— that is discipline.
— Bhagavad Gita

Would you live with ease? Do what you ought, and not what you please.
— Benjamin Franklin

What is true discipline?

True discipline is self-discipline. It was self-discipline that was inculcated in the *ashramas* of ancient India. The teacher– the Guru— was not a task-master. He encouraged students to develop self-discipline. You see, the teacher is not always with us, but we are always with ourselves. If we are trained to be disciplined, we will always be disciplined.

Therefore, we were taught that there is One who is watching us all the time. God is watching us. God is watching over us. Today, all this is forgotten. Even if God is a hypothesis, as so many people today declare, He is a very helpful hypothesis. But, God is not a mere hypothesis. God is real. God is actual.

How can young people cultivate self-discipline?

When Benjamin Franklin was a boy, he divided his day and night into compartments of fifteen minutes each. Every hour had four compartments and twenty four hours yielded ninety six compartments. Then he said, "So many compartments, I will devote to sleep, so many compartments, I will give to looking after the body. So many compartments, I will give to eating, so many compartments, I will give to studying. So many compartments, I will give to games." He led a disciplined life as a boy. Benjamin Franklin did not waver from the programme he had fixed for himself. Our way may not be the way of Benjamin Franklin— that was just an example. But, we must live a life of discipline.

I think that discipline is lacking in our lives. Discipline is conspicuous by its absence. There is no discipline in the home. There is no discipline in the school. In the home, the girl turns thirteen and the parents dare not ask, "Where are you going?" I was in London and the parents said, "We want to set a curfew for our daughter." They

Liberat... Egoism Violen...
...Seeker Service Silence Sp...
...rations Willpower Woman ...
...Of The World Bhagavad ...
...Selfishness, Frustration, ...
...Rituals Jadhu Vaswani ...
...Thought-Power Understanding
...Education Faith Fea...
...Meditati

said to her, "You have to come home by 11:30 p.m." She laughed, saying, "How can I come home before 11:30 p.m.? Our programmes commence at 11:30 p.m." The girl returned at 2:30 in the morning. She did not listen to her parents. There is no discipline.

In our days, we dared not come home a minute later than 8:30 in the night. For you, 8:30 is not even the beginning of having fun. We were not allowed to go to the movies. You may be surprised to know that until I did may post-graduation, I had seen just one movie: it was called Ben Hur. We were not allowed to touch playing cards. I don't even know how to shuffle a pack of playing cards. In those days, we had discipline in our families, in our schools, with our teachers. Today, teachers are afraid of their students. The whole world has become topsy-turvy. Values have gone mad.

What is freedom?

Freedom is not that you can do what you like. Freedom is to be able to do what you ought to do, what you should do.

How can we be alert and cultivate self-control and self-discipline?

This has to be a process. It can't be accomplished overnight or in a moment. In the *Upanishads*, the *rishis* tell us that at every step in every round of life, we are given a choice. Do we want to follow the path of *preya* (pleasant) or the path of *shreya* (good). The path of *preya* is a smooth, slippery path, but it can lead to our doom. The path of *shreya* is a stony and a thorny path, sometimes paved with flames, but it leads us to our good. We must grow in the path of self-discipline. This means that you have to make the right choice and stick to it whatever may be the conditions.

Duty

It is thy duty oftentimes to do what thou wouldst not;
thy duty, too, to leave undone that thou wouldst do.
— *Thomas A. Kempis*

Theirs not to make reply,
Theirs not to reason why,
Theirs but to do and die.
— *Tennyson*

There is no joy in doing one's own duty badly
Than in doing another man's duty well.
— *Bhagavad Gita*

How can we best do our duty?

There was a group of people who were doing some construction work. As long as the overseer was on the site, the workers were doing their duty. But, the moment he left, all of them left their work. This overseer happened to have an artificial eye, so the next time he left, he took that eye and kept it on the table saying, "This eye will be watching you." Then one of the labourers had an idea. He took off his cap and placed it over the eye.

This is what we are doing. Duties are forgotten today. Nowadays, if we ask somebody, "Why don't you do your duty?" They reply, "I don't get any pleasure out of it." As the Master unfolds his doctrine of *Karma* in the *Bhagavad Gita*, he says to Arjuna that the very first thing you must note is devotion to duty. The *Gita* calls it *Swadharma*. "Do your duty, O Arjuna!" An English poet says, "I slept and dreamt that life was beauty. I woke and found that life was duty." Nowadays, it is beauty that draws people. Learning to do one's duty is a matter of discipline.

If we have to renounce the results, why do we require the process of working?

Work is not an end in itself, it is only a means. Work is a means to self-purification. I am doing my work, with this in view that my interior self may be purified. That is the purpose of work. And that self-purification will come about only if I work and accept whatever result the Super Power sends me. Work is not an end in itself. Work is a means to self-purification.

Many people think that everything is in their hands. Therefore, they are not able to accept the results. But, let me tell you that according to the teaching of the *Gita*, every work has five causes. Four causes are in man's hands—the doer, the field of work, the know-how and the implements of work. The *Gita* says, there is a fifth factor which is not in the hands of man. The *Gita* calls it *adrishta*. *Adrishta* means the unseen.

For example, a peasant plows the land, sows the seed at the right time. But then he has to wait for the rains to fall. Now if the rains do not fall and the seed dries up, there can be no crop. There are two options open to the peasant—either to break his head against the wall, to weep, to tear his hair, call his family members and tell them to do likewise or to be positive and say, "There must be some good in it. Lord, I accept. But I am not going to give up this work. I am going to do it in the next season." Which is the better option?

In today's world of competition, we see that the man who is clever is able to win over his rivals. If we practise honesty, it does not seem to pay. Lord Krishna explains in the Gita to Arjuna, that he must use all means to win, as he cannot afford to lose the battle. What do we do?

Lord Krishna does not ask us to do anything to win the battle. I think the confusion has arisen out of this mistaken notion that work is the end. Work is not an end in itself, it is only a means. The end is different. You have to decide your own goals and your own end. If your end is to be the richest man in the world, then your work will be along that direction. According to the *Gita*, the goal should be Self-realisation, God-realisation. But according to you, it may be different. But in the achieving of our goals, we must not forget, that our means should be pure. For instance, Mahatma Gandhi placed before India the goal of independence. But Mahatma Gandhi was very careful to point out that in the achievement of that goal, in the achievement of independence, we must see that our means are pure and honest. That must not be forgotten. If my goal is wealth but my means are impure and if I achieve the goal, all the money that I have will be soiled money. It will not be clean money and soiled money will never give you happiness, soiled money will never give you peace of mind.

The goal of life should be that which should make us happy, and at peace with all. For that, the means have to be pure and honest. This is the teaching of the *Bhagavad Gita*.

Education

A child miseducated is a child lost.
— John F. Kennedy

Education is, essentially, a thing of the Spirit.
— Sadhu Vaswani

Education is not the filling of a pail, but the lighting of a fire.
— William Butler Yeats

If a man empties a purse into his head, no one can take it from him.
— Benjamin Franklin

What is your opinion of education in our age?

Current education is dissatisfied with itself; and the dissatisfaction grows more and more. As witnesses to this dissatisfaction, we have student unrest in India and other countries of the world. Universities are being burnt, vice-chancellors are being *gheraoed*, teachers are being threatened and mishandled.

"Judge a tree by its fruits," said a great teacher of Palestine. Judged by its fruits, current education has failed miserably. This education must go. A new type of education is needed— an education related to real life. Education must not be merely academic or abstract. It must not aim at stuffing the student with information acquired from dead books or a set of sterile moralities and superficial values. True education should equip the student to cope adequately with life, with what lies ahead of him so that he may become a worthy participant in the adventure of life.

Why are students disillusioned with the system of education?

Students are no longer happy with the learning of books which have no relation to real life. Nor are they interested in examinations which elevate text-books to the status of scriptures. They want answers to the pressing problems of life—problems which confront them in their day-to-day existence. They are eager to find out ways by which the world may be changed into a better, nobler, happier place. For no apparent fault of theirs, they find themselves in a world of injustice and exploitation, of cruelty and cut-throat competition, of hypocrisy and cant, of poverty and pain. And to their deep regret they find that the so-called elders take things for granted and do nothing to remedy the tragic situation.

What is the right way to educate our children?

Educate them, first and foremost, to know God and love Him. The trouble with most of our schools and colleges today is that God has been divorced from our education. Make God a reality to your child, and you will find that he grows in those true qualities of character without which life has no meaning or significance.

How can we achieve a real change in our education system?

To bring about a real change in the educational system, what we need are teachers of the true type. Teachers who will teach, through precept and example, that life is larger than livelihood and that the end of knowledge is not gains in silver and gold, jobs and careers, but sympathy, service, and sacrifice.

What according to you, is the most ideal gift a teacher could give to a pupil and a pupil could give to a teacher?

I think that the ideal gift a teacher can give to a pupil is friendship. And the ideal gift that a pupil can give to the teacher is, of course, reverence. We have a whole doctrine of knowledge unfolded in the *Gita*. The Lord, speaking unto his disciple, Arjuna, says, there are three things every pupil must do if he wants to walk on the path of wisdom. The very first thing he calls *paripatenah*, the second is *prashnena*, and the third is *sevaya*. The first is *paripatenah*, that is reverence. The student must approach the teacher in a spirit of reverence. Then *prashnena*, whatever be his or her doubt, he must come and place it before the teacher. The third is *sevaya*, he must serve the guru, or the teacher with his own hands. Indeed, there was a time when the pupils used to press the legs of their teachers. Now, if the teacher asks them to press his leg, they may pinch his leg, instead!

How can we make this spirit of reverence grow?

For this, teachers of the true type are needed. Can you ever imagine teachers going on strike for higher wages? Today, teaching is regarded as a profession, rather than a vocation. What impact will such teachers have on the minds of the students? We need teachers of a new type who, through precept and example, will impress upon the pupils that life is larger than livelihood.

What is character?

The literal meaning of the word 'character' is carving and engraving. Character is that which is to be engraved in the plastic minds of the pupils. Sow within them the seeds of character, the seeds of simplicity and service, of purity and prayer. This was the four-fold motto which Sadhu Vaswani gave to the Mira School, simplicity and service, purity and prayer.

Dada, Sadhu Vaswani laid great stress on education; why?

Sadhu Vaswani believed that what we need are men and women of character, men and women of sterling qualities, who may take charge of the administration, and who may be in charge of different spheres of our activities. "New India," he said, "will not be built in the Loksabha or Rajyasabha, but new India will be built in the home and in the school." Therefore give your children the right type of training in the home, and the right type of education in the school.

Can you tell us something about the Mira Movement in education?

In the Mira schools, and college which are situated at Pune and at some other cities in India, we are putting forth an humble effort in the direction of giving the right type of education to our students. In these institutions, our teachers are putting forth their best efforts to train students to show commendable results at the board and the university examinations, but the emphasis is not on passing examinations, but on other things.

I love to call them the five fingers of education. The very first finger of education is character-building. Is it not true that the one urgent, the one piteous need of India today, is men and women of character? It is true, India needs foreign exchange and the goods which foreign exchange can buy. India needs technical know-how and a new social and economic planning. But more than all these things put together, India needs men and women of character. Men and women whom the lust of office will not betray, whom the gains of office will not lead astray, who will not scramble for power, but who will use all their power, in a spirit of humility, in the service of India's teeming millions.

Secondly, our emphasis is on what we call *seva*— the quality of service. We believe that character is best built through altruistic living, living for others. Therefore, the children are trained to forget themselves and spend their energies in giving comfort to those that are in need of comfort, in bringing joy into the lives of those that are joyless.

Thirdly, the emphasis is on Indian ideals. Modern scientific knowledge is passed on to the students but they are asked not to forget their rich heritage— the heritage which belongs to them as children of the ancient *rishis*. It is only with a blend of modern scientific knowledge and India's ancient wisdom that a new civilisation can be built.

In the fourth place, the emphasis is on international understanding.

In the fifth place, the emphasis is on cultivation of the soul. Man, is essentially, a soul. Our great blunder is that we have identified ourselves with the body that we wear, or, at best with the body-mind complex. But man is essentially a soul. Cultivate the soul.

When does education begin?

Education is pre-natal. While the child is in the womb, the mother must think sublime thoughts. She must have no thoughts of resentment, ill-will, jealousy, against anyone as this will influence the child in the womb.

A woman came to a sage and said to him, "My child is just born. When do I start educating him?" The sage told her, "You have already wasted nine months."

What is the secret of education?

Reverence is the secret of education. Tennyson has said, "Let knowledge grow from more to more, but more of reverence in us dwell."

Reverence is of three types— reverence for what is above us, for what is beneath us and for what is around us.

Faith

Faith is the bird that sings when the dawn is still dark.
– Rabindranath Tagore

So on I go, not knowing
I would not, if I might;
I'd rather walk in the dark with God
Then go alone in the light;
I'd rather walk by faith with Him,
Than go alone by sight.
– Anonymous

Faith sees the invisible, believes the incredible, and receives the impossible
– Anonymous

There are some occasions in life, which tend to shake our faith in the Almighty. How should we develop unflinching faith in the Lord?

Suppose there is a storm. It will uproot all the shrubs and plants but will not be able to uproot the mighty trees that have strong roots. Storms of the changing vicissitudes of life blow over us. If our roots are firm, those storms will not be able to uproot us. Because our roots are not firm, certain things happen and we lose our faith in God. We have to strengthen our roots.

How may the roots of faith become firm?

Firstly, by associating with people whose faith is strong.

Secondly, daily self-analysis helps in building faith.

Thirdly, a little of meditation.

Fourthly, a little of selfless service.

Fifthly, constant prayer. These are the things that build up our faith, build up our roots.

What is it to seek refuge in God?

To seek refuge is to trust in the Lord—fully, completely, entirely. It is to know that He is the One Light that shines and shines and ever shines. Though the storms howl and the darkness grows deeper, His light shines on! He is the creator and the nourisher of all that is, He is the deliverer from whom all evils flee. He is nearer to us than our heartbeats and closer than our breathing. He is the all-powerful One whose hands are everywhere. He is sufficient as a friend, sufficient as a helper. There is not a corner too remote for His help to reach us. He is the all-loving One whose ears are ever attentive to the prayers of His wayward children. He is the all-knowing One who does the very best for us. With Him all things are possible: and if He chooses not to do certain things which we want Him to do, it is not because He cannot do them, but because He knows that they are not for our good. So it is that he who hath found his refuge in the Lord is ever ready and willing to do God's Will. "Not my will but Thine be done, O Lord !" he prays again and again.

Tell us about surrender.

The one lesson we all need to learn is—utter dependence upon God. Everything else will follow. We must turn to God for every little thing we need—until, one blessed day, we find that we need nothing: our one and only need is God! Then we make the great discovery that all that we need is already provided for. Before a need arises, it is already fulfilled. Everything comes to pass at the right time, in the right way. Then one lives like a king. When a king moves out, everything is prepared for him well in advance, he does not have to ask for anything. All his needs are anticipated and provided for.

"Ye are kings! Why wander ye like the kings' children, who starved and were clothed in rags, because they were unaware of their royal parentage?"

What are the marks of a man who has surrendered his will to the Will of the Lord?

He who seeks refuge in the Lord, becomes a servant of the Will divine. He welcomes not gain, he fears not loss. He desires not pleasure, he runs not away from pain. He seeks not success, nor does he avoid failure. He accepts all that comes to him as a gift from the Lord who loves him and whom he loves. And he finds that life is the great guru, the great teacher, the great initiator. Every experience enriches his interior life, leads him onward in the march of the true, the good, the beautiful and the holy. Every pain makes him perfect, every suffering makes him strong.

He whose refuge is the Lord, lives in constant awareness of God's presence. Such a man is never alone, Another is always with him, blessing him, guiding him, protecting him, leading him on! He hears His gentle voice: he feels the warm pressure of His hand on his. He hearkens to the voice of his unseen Friend, and he always feels safe and secure even in the face of danger and death.

Fear

Nothing in life is to be feared, it is only to be understood.
— Marie Curie

*All things fear him who fears God, while he who fears nothing else but God
is in fear of all things.*
— Attar

There would be no one to frighten you if you refused to be afraid.
— Mohandas K. Gandhi

Why do we become victims of fear?

Fear—is the one mark which characterises us, children of a sceptical age. We are afraid of the future, afraid of poverty, afraid of unemployment, afraid of dishonour and disgrace, afraid of disease and death—afraid even of life! We live in constant fear of losing what little we have.

I know of a woman who has a small metal box with a little gold in it. She stayed as our guest for some weeks. She spent sleepless nights often getting up to see if her gold was intact. She was afraid, lest someone pilfered her gold under cover of the night! We live in fear, we work in fear, we walk in fear, we talk in fear. We move through life from one fear to another, crushed beneath the weight of a woeful existence.

How may we overcome fear?

Fear is a child of unfaith. He who lives in fear does not truly believe in God, howsoever much he may have the Name of God on his lips. The man who believes in God is released from the bondage of fear and ego-centredness. The worst may happen to him: he is unafraid. Misfortune may follow him as a faithful dog: but he is unafraid. Poverty and pestilence may stare him in the face, yet he is unafraid. Imprisoned in a dark cell, taken to the gallows, thrown into the midst of ferocious beasts, he is still fearless, brave, unafraid. For he has given himself over to an all-loving and all-wise God. No longer does he belong to himself: he belongs to God. It is God's sole responsibility to look after him, to guard him against all pitfalls, to provide for him. There can be nothing better than what God wills for him. So, in every situation and circumstance of life, he gives praise to and glorifies the Lord and utters the one word of gratitude, "*Shukur!* *Shukur!*"

tion Life ..ism, Violent Dreams.. ..gism, Service Silence Spirituality Willpower Woman Yoga.. ..Of The World Bhagavad Gita G.. ..eeker Vibrations Willpower Woman Yoga.. ..Selflessness, Frustration, Worry.. ..Rituals Sadhu Vaswani Science.. ..Thought Power Understanding Fo.. ..Education Faith Fear Forg.. ..Meditation Mi.. ..And G

Why is it that the vast majority of us live perpetually in fear of something or the other?

Perhaps, one reason is that we are lonely. The deepest tragedy of modern man is his loneliness. In spite of an ever-increasing number of clubs and cinemas, museums and parks, hotels and restaurants, at heart we feel lonely.

A distinguished visitor to America was taken to a big cinema house. Throngs of people stood in rows awaiting their turn to get a ticket. Asked for his opinion, the visitor said, "The Americans must be very lonely at heart, otherwise there would not be endless queues at cinema houses!"

Yes—if we will confess the truth to ourselves we will not deny that we feel lonely. We lack the security of protection. We are like the child, who, taken to a fair, has lost its mother in the crowd. With this difference that the child rent the air with its cries for the mother, "Ma! Ma!" But we have forgotten even to cry for our divine Mother. We are like the orphan who was never tired of complaining that there was no one to care for him in this big, boisterous world.

It is this sense of loneliness that leads to a feeling of frustration, and so, many of us do not find it worth while to live in the world. Not long ago, a multi-millionaire ended his life after leaving a brief note on his writing-table, "I feel lonely. Therefore, I kill myself!"

Life is becoming a burden to untold millions. Only a few commit suicide. The rest die what are regarded as natural deaths but which are, in many cases, too premature. So many feel lonely, and loneliness sits as a heavy burden on the heart, sapping its strength, eating into its vitals. Heart diseases are on the increase, hypertension has become a common ailment, nervous breakdowns take a heavy toll.

We feel lonely, and lost. We feel abandoned, forsaken and forlorn. Again and again, we lose the sense of security which belongs to us as children of God, we fall into the abyss of fear.

How can we protect ourselves when fear strikes us?

Fear is a poison that quickly circulates through the entire system, paralysing the will, producing a queer sensation in some part or the other of the human body. Fear is the great foe of man.

Overcome fear the moment it appears or it will overpower you. And fear is a merciless master. Strike fear with the weapon of the Spirit—the Word, God. Utter the sacred Name dear to you, the Name of the beloved—Krishna, Shyama, Jesus, Buddha, Nanak. Utter it, again and again. Utter it in childlike faith, and He, whom you call will rush to your aid. Say aloud some prayer which appeals to your heart.

Give us a few practical tips on overcoming fear.

Here are seven steps on the road that leads from fear to fearlessness:

1. Convince yourself that nothing that you fear is as bad as the fear itself. To be afraid is the worst thing that can happen to you.

2. Be sure you want to give up the thing you are afraid of. You must have the will to be free.

3. Never forget that fear is a kind of atheism.

4. Remember, that with God all things are possible.

5. To receive the power of God, learn to relax in His presence.

6. Do not be afraid of what may happen tomorrow.

7. Go out of yourself and bring help and comfort to others.

Forgiveness

*Forgiveness is the fragrance the violent sheds
on the heel that has crushed it.*
— Anonymous

*He that cannot forgive others breaks the bridge over
which he must pass himself; for every man has need to be forgiven.*
— Thomas Fuller, M.D.

Forgive others often, yourself never.
— Syrus

How can we develop the spirit of forgiveness?

To walk the way of forgiveness, one has to pass through four stages. The first is the stage of hurt. Someone has wronged me, done something mean to me, been unfair to me: and I cannot forget it. I feel hurt. The hurt keeps on pricking me as a thorn. It is here that we must remember that it is not I who feel hurt, but the ego. Those that are at this stage naturally hold grudges, not realising that the person who holds a grudge injures himself more than the one against whom the grudge is held.

Hatred and malice, like anger and worry, bring harm to the body, since they poison the blood. And they keep on increasing for, "a grudge is the only thing that does not get better when it is nursed."

Hurt leads to hate which is the second stage. I cannot forget how much I have been hurt and I cannot send out thoughts of goodwill to my enemy. In some cases, I hate the person so much that I want him or her to suffer, as much as I am suffering.

Then comes the third stage: it is the stage of healing. God's grace descends on me and I begin to see the person who hurt me in a new light. I begin to understand his or her difficulty. My memory is healed and I am free again.

The fourth is the stage of coming together. I am anxious to make friends with the person who has hurt me. I invite him into my life. I share my love with him and we both move to a new and healed relationship.

Dada, can we develop the spirit of forgiveness you speak of?

What I call 'the ten fingers of forgiveness' are actually practical suggestions on how to walk the way of forgiveness.

When anyone Life ... Violent Dream ... Spiritual ... Woman Yoga
... Service Silence ... Of The World Bhagavad Gita ... Worry ... Science
Vibrations Willpower ... Selfishness, Frustration ... Understanding
... Rituals Sadhu Vaswani ... Education Faith Fear Forgi
... Thought Power ... Meditation Mi
And Gl

1. When anyone hurts you, immediately offer a prayer to God, "O God, help me to forget this hurt so that it does not enter my heart, and become a festering wound."

2. If someone has hurt you to a point where you are unable to forget it, unburden yourself to a spiritual elder, or write a letter to the person against whom you hold a grudge.

3. Learn to forgive yourself— do not carry the burden of guilt in your heart.

4. Never hold resentment against anyone in the heart within. This can only harm you.

5. Every night as you retire, think of all the people who have wronged you or hurt you, actually call out their names aloud and say, "I forgive you."

6. Make forgiveness a habit. It is not enough to forgive once or twice or thrice. We must keep on forgiving as often as we are wronged.

7. Go one step further— forgive even before forgiveness is asked.

8. When you forgive, make sure that you forget.

9. Speak kindly about the person against whom you hold a grudge.

10. Rise above your resentment and actually love the person who has wronged you.

Friendship

The only way to have a friend is to be one.
– Ralph Waldo Emerson

I went out to find a friend
But did not find one there
I went out to be a friend
And friends were everywhere
– Author Unknown

Friends are angels who lift us to our feet when our wings have trouble
remembering how to fly
– Anonymous

Who is a true friend?

A friend is one who knows my faults and failings, my weaknesses and my imperfections, my oddities and whims— and still loves me.

What do you give to a friend?

You give to a friend the love of your heart and good, chaste advice.

What do you take from a friend?

Nothing. Otherwise, you are not a friend. If you think of taking from a friend, then you are not a friend. To be a true friend you have to be a giver.

How may we nourish friendship?

1. Permit your friends to be themselves. Accept them as they are. Accept each one's imperfections.

2. Let there be space between you and your friend. Let him have his privacy and you your own.

3. Be eager to help your friend. A friend in need is a friend indeed.

4. Make your advice constructive. Do not give advice until asked for.

5. Be loyal—this means being with your friend in bad times as well as good.

6. Give praise. Tell your friends what you like about them and be thankful to them for their presence in your life.

7. Be honest. Express your feelings. Do not bottle your anger or your anxiety. Clearing the air helps relationships to grow. But be aware that sometimes, things are better left unsaid.

8. Trust your friends. Never doubt their goodness.

How may we recognise a true friend?

There are the three marks of a true friend:

1.   If he finds you moving on the path of evil, he will do all he can to set your feet on the path of righteousness.

2.   He is not a flatterer. He will tell you the truth even at the cost of incurring your displeasure.

3.   When you are in trouble or in need, he will be the first to rush to your help.

Future of the World

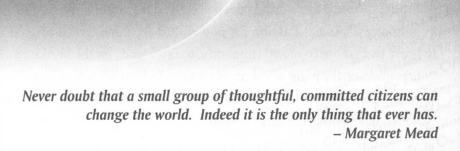

Never doubt that a small group of thoughtful, committed citizens can change the world. Indeed it is the only thing that ever has.
— Margaret Mead

There will be no peace so long as
God remains unseated at the conference table.
— William M. Peck

The condition of mankind at present, is difficult. What do you think needs to be done to make the world new?

Let me tell you of Solon, one of the seven wise men of ancient Greece. On one occasion, he carried a rotten apple in his hand, asking each one he met the same question, "How can this apple be renewed?"

Nobody could answer the question. What can be done with a rotten apple, people thought. Thereafter, Solon cut the apple, took out the seeds and told them, "If these seeds are sown in the soil, we will have new apples growing from the tree."

The seeds of mankind are little children. Let us take care of them. Let us impart to them a new education which will sow in their tender hearts the seeds of character and compassion— and mankind will be come anew.

Is there hope for the world, Dada?

The world today is passing through a period of crisis. Unrest in all the countries of the world is deepening and nations are moving in a jungle of darkness. Passion for power, lust for fame, greed of gold, grow from more to more. Humanity, today, stands on the brinks of a precipice, on the point of committing suicide. Humanity, today, is like an orphan crying in the night; crying for the light. It is the light of understanding that the nations need.

Today, we have arrived at a stage where, nations and individuals alike must learn to understand one another or perish. There is no other choice!

They say bigger is better, do you agree?

Today, there is, among the nations, a wild race for rockets and space-ships, and satellites which have only a brief, whirling existence. Today, there is a craze for bigness, for greatness. Little things do not satisfy us any more. Our egos are inflated. We are anxious to become builders of big institutions, founders of big organisations, writers of big volumes. This craze leads us to big unhappiness. For bigness is a mirage. Many run after it, and their thirst continues to grow from more and more until, they drop down dead!

What do you think is the need of Europe and America?

The one need of Europe and America, as it is of India and Russia and Africa and all other countries of the world—our one urgent need—is the child-heart, the heart of a child. Of such, said Jesus, is the Kingdom of heaven, the Kingdom of happiness. We are becoming more and more clever—perhaps, crafty and cunning—in our individual, national and international dealings. We wish to outwit the other person or nation. The world needs straightforward people.

God, give us men of faith, wisdom and love, of sympathy and simplicity and service! God, give us men who have the child-heart. They will lead the nations out of darkness into light! They will usher in a new era of peace for which the wounded, the tortured soul of humanity has piteously cried through the ages.

Why is there such moral decay in the world?

To this question there can be a variety of answers which may lead to endless and futile discussions. The fact is that there is moral decay. So let me do the little I can, to dispel the darkness around me. Let me kindle, in my own life, a little candle of purity, simplicity, selfless service. To reform the world, Sadhu Vaswani said, begin with yourself!

To begin with myself, what would you advise me to do?

Four things: firstly, hand yourself over to the Lord. Turn over your life in childlike trust to the Lord.

Secondly, rejoice in everything that the Will of God brings to you. Whatever happens in the divine providence, happens for our good. So wherever God keep me, let me remain. Wherever He sends me, let me go.

Thirdly, let me spend some time everyday in silence, in prayer, in meditation, in silent study of spiritual truths. I often refer to it as our daily appointment with God.

And, fourthly, let me help others. Sadhu Vaswani said to us, "Did you meet him on the road? Did you leave him with the load?" The day on which I have not helped a brother here, a sister there, to lift the load on the rough road of life, is a lost day indeed.

What is the final destiny of the human being?

In simple words I would say, the final destiny of each and every human being is to attain perfection. Did not Jesus tell us, "Be ye perfect, even as thy Father in heaven is perfect." There he indicates the final destiny of every individual. Life is a journey to perfection.

We go through a series of experiences when we are born on this earth—and each experience teaches us something. I would say life is like a school, a college or a university, and experiences are our teachers. I need to learn certain lessons, and so I have been sent to this earthplane. Each one of us has to learn a different set of lessons, and so each one of us goes through a different set of experiences. But each experience comes to teach me a valuable lesson, and take me one step ahead towards perfection.

What is the greatest danger of our planet, today?

The great danger of our planet today is not merely from environmental pollution, but also from mental, and spiritual pollution. Today, the moral base of public life has been shattered. Values have gone mad. The world seems to be falling apart, terrorism is everywhere. And drug abuse and alcoholism are destroying our youth. What will save our sinking civilisation is a new spiritual awakening—a new education—a new religion of reverence for all life.

Do you believe we are on the threshold of a new age?

Not merely believe, I can almost hear the new age knocking on the doors of our hearts. Where are the blessed ones who will open the door to the new age?

For thousands of years, nations have fought one another—and look at what man has made of man. We are standing on the threshold of a new age of love which will bring brotherhood among all nations and people.

When will this happen? How will it happen?

Let me tell you that within nature there is only development. Time and space are human qualities. The new age will come when the old has lived to the full. First, a great broom will sweep out all old values and ideals (and that is what we are witnessing today) and new values and ideals will arise in the hearts of men. Then the new age of love and peace will be established on earth.

What changes will the new age bring in?

As the new age dawns, materialism will automatically lag behind spirituality. And people will live the *Vedanta* in their daily lives. The *Vedantic* concept is spiritual. One life flows in all things. Therefore the future civilisation will be built on reverence for life. All life is sacred. Therefore in your day-to-day living, show reverence for everything—the earth, sky, trees, stones, rivers, animals, flowers. The *Vedantic* concept is spiritual yet scientific, for scientists tell us that there is life even in a stone and that the molecules in a stone are ever changing. Now the time has come when man must either make friends with nature or perish. This is the truth.

When will the new world order come?

All over the world, today, there is a cry for a new world order, a new life, for men and women, boys and girls are tired of the present order of things. The cry comes from temples and churches, from farms and factories, from homes and offices, and from hearts full of aspiration and love.

What is the secret of the new life? Contact with the beloved within the heart. Out of this inner contact will flow the waters of life, and the old order will be washed away, yielding place to the new.

How can we bring in this new world order?

We can usher in this new world order by developing a sense of fellowship, kinship with all—we, rich and poor, prince and peasant, belong to the one fellowship. We are all one! For the one Divine Spirit is the indwelling spirit of all.

St. Louis was the king of France. Clad as a poor pilgrim, he came, one day, to meet Brother Giles who lived in the Franciscan monastery. Brother Giles met his royal guest with love. Each embraced the other. Then both knelt together in silent prayer. Not a word passed between them. After about two hours of prayerful silence, King Louis rose from his knees and returned to his palace.

The brother-monks of Giles reproached him, saying, "The king was your guest and you spoke to him not a single word of welcome!"

And Giles answered in utter simplicity, "There was no need to speak, I read his heart; and he read mine!"

Giles was a poor monk. Louis was a rich ruler of France. They both realised that they belong to one fellowship.

This fellowship—of heart with heart—Sadhu Vaswani says, is deeper than political democracy.

Secondly, through reverent communion with the mystery of the earth, the sun and the stars, and with the saints and heroes of the east and west.

Thirdly, through love for little children.

In these three are the seeds of the new world order, which is a piteous need of our excited, agitated age.

What is your vision of the 21st century?

My vision is very simple. It is a vision of a world without war, a world without want. A world in which every human being, irrespective of country, colour, and creed, gets the necessities of life and is able to hold his head high. A world in which peace prevails among nations and harmony among the peoples of the earth. A world in which the right to live is granted to every creature that breathes the breath of life. It is the vision of a world in which the truth is recognised that life and all its bounties, all that we are and have— our time and talents, knowledge and wisdom, experience and influence, prestige and power, wealth and strength, indeed, life itself, is a loan given to us, to be passed on to those whose need is greater than ours.

How can we bring about peace on earth?

Wars will not leave the face of this earth until we have peace in our hearts. "How can there be peace on earth when the hearts of men are a volcano?" said Sadhu Vaswani. Understanding and love are pre-conditions of world peace.

But just as some people are short-sighted or far-sighted and often their vision is clouded, similarly our vision is obscured from our very birth by prejudices of family, race and nation. Break these barriers and realise the truth that all the children of the earth are one. The key to peace is to love one another unconditionally. Love the world as your own nation, as your own sibling.

Bhagavad Gita

The Gita is the Ganges of Light—
a River of radiance running from Eternity to Time!
— Sadhu Vaswani

Dada, tell us a little about the Bhagavad Gita?

The *Bhagavad Gita* is a very tiny fragment of the 6th canto of the great India's epic—the *Mahabharata*. The *Mahabharata* was written by Ved Vyas—a great sage of India. He is regarded as the *Adi* Guru, the first Guru, the guru of all gurus in India. He has compiled the four *Vedas*, he has written the 18 *Puranas*, the *Brahma Sutra* and the *Mahabharata*.

It was on the battlefield of *Kurukshetra*, standing in the midst of the raging armies of the *Pandavas* and *Kauravas*, that *Sri* Krishna gave utterance to that great teaching which the centuries have revered as the *Bhagavad Gita*.

The *Gita* is said to consist of 701 *slokas*, but for some reason or the other, one of the *slokas* does not bear a number at all. The *Gita* is a book of eighteen chapters—18 *adhyayas* as we call them.

What is the literal meaning of the word Gita?

The literal meaning of the word *Gita*, is a song. And the Gita is essentially a song of life. An important note that enters into the song of life is suffering, is sorrow, is pain— *Vishada* as the *Gita* calls it. The very opening chapter of the *Gita* is entitled *Vishada Yoga*.

What is Vishada Yoga?

Arjuna is in *Vishada*. He comes to the battlefield full of valour and the thought of victory. He is the hero of a hundred battles. He is confident that he will be victorious in this battle also, especially as Sri Krishna is by his side. But, as he takes his place in the midst of the ranging armies, as he surveys the opposing camp of the *Kauravas* and sees there his own kinsmen, his cousins, friends and teachers, his *acharyas* and his *Guru*— his heart is dismayed. Arjuna gets suddenly depressed. His mind is confused. In a state of utter helplessness he says to Sri Krishna, "Krishna, my limbs fail, my body quivers, my

Dada we are told that a sinner is doomed to burn in the fires of hell for ever. Does the Gita also says so?

Theologians frighten us with the thought that the sinner is doomed to burn in the fires of hell and these fires will never be quenched. But, Sri Krishna says in the *Gita*: "I am seated in the hearts of all." He is seated in the hearts of sinners as he is seated in the hearts of saints. It is only that the saint can reveal Sri Krishna better than the sinner because of the purity of his life.

Sri Krishna taught: "Repent, repent, repent, and with one single tear you can quench the fires of hell." He also said, "The sinner is not doomed to eternal punishment for, within the sinner, too, there dwells the eternal beloved." Sadhu Vaswani said: "The sinner of today, may be a saint of tomorrow."

Do not chastise the sinner. Do not look down upon him. Do not hold him in contempt. Do not criticise him. But continue to pour upon him the pure, passionless love of your heart and he will come back.

We have these wonderful words in the *Bhagavad Gita*—Chapter 9—*slokas* 30 and 31. The Lord says, "Even if a man, deep sunk in sin, worships me in single devotion, he will soon become righteous and reach everlasting peace."

What is the essential message of the Gita?

Libraries of books have been written on the teachings of the *Gita* but they have not been able to exhaust its great message. Every year, new commentaries are being published. We cannot read all these books, and even if we were to read them, we would be unable to understand many of the philosophical thoughts they contain.

You have all heard of Sri Ramkrishna Paramhansa, one of the greatest saints of modern India. One day, his disciples said to him,

"Master, give us the essential teaching of the *Gita* in a few simple words." Sri Ramkrishna says to them, "I will give you the answer in one simple word. Repeat the word *Gita* ten times, and you will hear the word, *tagi*. *Tagi* is *tyagi*, and *tyagi* is a man of renunciation".

Does this mean that we have to renounce this world?

True renunciation is not outer. We do not have to wear ochre robes. We do not have to leave the obligations and enter into the depths of the *tapobana*— a forest of meditation. We have to be in the world but not be of the world. Once again, it was Sri Ramkrishna who said, "The boat must stay on the waters. But the waters must not be allowed to enter the boat, else the boat will sink and we will get drowned." Likewise, the boats of our lives must float on the waters of worldliness. We have to live in the world and perform our duties. But we must not let the waters of worldliness enter our boats.

Dada, what is the relation between the Gita and the Upanishads?

The *Gita* is rightly regarded as the milk of the *Upanishads*. The *Gita* emphasises the two-fold teaching which is the essence of the *Upanishads*: 1. Unity of life. All life is one. The forms are many, but the life that flows into them all is one! Caste, community, colour are accidental. The essential thing is that One life flows into all, making us all one. 2. The one life manifests itself in three ways: (i) in nature; (ii) in the heart of man; and (iii) in the great ones who appear— age after age, in the procession of history– not great in temporal power and possessions, but great in renunciation and service.

Is it necessary to read or recite the Gita every day?

The *Gita's* emphasis is on life. Not he who chants *sloka*s from the *Gita*, nor even he who delivers illuminating discourses on the *Gita*, but he who lives in accordance with the teachings of the *Gita* is dear to the Lord. The name of Krishna may be on my lips, but if my life does not bear witness to the Lord of love; if my heart does not throb in sympathy with those who are in suffering and pain; if I do not share what I have with the poor and needy; I am far from the Light.

How should we perform our duties according to the teachings of the Gita?

All around us today, there is confusion and chaos, for the people are out to assert their rights. No one thinks of doing his or her duty. When the emphasis is shifted from rights to duties, when each one does his or her own duty, then indeed, will India become new. The *Gita* teaches us that we must do our duty, and do it without expecting anything in return. Do your duty for the pure love of God.

Dada how can we practise the teaching of the Gita in our daily life?

To put the teaching of the *Gita* into practice, you must:

1. Begin the day with practice of silence. In the midst of your daily work, repeat to yourself, again and again some *sloka* of the *Gita*.

2. Never be idle for a single moment, but do what you can to serve those in suffering and pain.

3. Never swerve from your path of duty.

4. Do everything for the love of God.

5. Do not run after prominence or power but always seek the lowest place.

Dada, what is raja yoga?

The *Gita* is a scripture of *yoga—raja yoga*. *Raja yoga* means the royal *yoga*. "Each one of you is royal. Each of you is a king!" proclaims the *Gita*. But, entering into this world of mud and matter, coming under the influences of the allurements and entanglements of this earth-plane, you have forgotten your true self, your divine destiny. And the *Gita* gives the great message, "Away with forgetfulness! Awake to remembrance! Recollect what you are! You are not the weakling you take yourself to be! Ye are kings! Within you lie locked up infinite powers of the Spirit, untold treasures of the Eternal. Set them free and you will find that the impossible becomes possible."

The way to unlock the hidden powers of the Spirit, is the way of yoga. And the *Gita*—*raja yoga*—is a synthesis of three *yogas*.

What are the three yogas that the Gita speaks of?

There is, firstly, *karma yoga*. I prefer to call it *dharma yoga*, the path to duty, way of selfless action. There is, secondly, *bhakti yoga* or *prema yoga*: I sometimes refer to it as *buddhi yoga*, the way of wisdom. The three must cooperate to attain perfection in life?

The call of *karma* or *dharma yoga* is, "to thine own duty be true!" Each one of us has his duty to perform, his obligations to fulfil. The father has his own duties to perform; the mother has hers. The teacher has his duties and the student has his. The labourer in a factory and the capitalist owner of the factory– each has his own duties. Today there is confusion, for, every one claims his rights; no one seems to think of his duties. And the *Gita* comes with the great message, this earth is a *karma-bhumi, a dharma-kshetra*—a plane of action, a field of duty. Do thy duty!

You do not have to enter the depths of a *tapovana*, a forest of meditation. You have to be in the world to fulfil your tasks. If only each one of us did his or her own duty, what a wonderful world it would be!

He, who would tread the path of duty, must take note of three things. The first is *daan*, giving. Life and all the bounties of life are given to you to be shared with those in need. Give, in the measure of your strength, to the poor and broken ones, the forsaken and forlorn.

Sadhu Vaswani, who was regarded by many as a "living *Gita*", often said to us, "the day on which you have not helped a brother here, or a sister there to lift the load on the rough road of life, is a lost day indeed!" Give, but not in pride. Give in reverence to the poor. For the poor are the pictures of God. And to serve them is to worship God.

An important teaching of the *Gita* given us in half a *sloka* in which the Master says, "He who cooks for himself alone is a thief!" Do I have in my house food only for myself and my family members? Then I am no better than a thief, or a robber. Before I eat my meals, I must set apart a share for the hungry or starving one—a man, a bird, an animal.

The second thing to be noted by him who would tread the path of duty is *yagna*—offering one's actions to the Lord. And the third thing is *tapas*, self-control, control of the senses. A man without self-control is no better than an animal—a prey to every passing excitement and sensation.

Tell us about bhakti yoga?

In the path of *bhakti* or *prema yoga*, there are likewise three steps. The first is *anuraga*, longing for the first and only fair, deep yearning for the Lord.

The second is *shraddha* or reverence for God and the guru who is a manifestation of God.

The third is *karuna*, compassion for all who suffer and are in pain, compassion for birds and animals, who, alas, are being slain by the million in our soulless cities everyday! One mark of *karuna* is simplicity. For the man of compassion will not indulge in a life of luxury when all around him is the poverty and starvation of millions. He will strive to serve the poor.

God

Fear that man who fears not God.
— Abd-el-Kader

Grasping without eyes, hasting without feet, He sees without eyes, he hears without ears. He knows what can be known, but not one knows Him.
— Upanishads

God defined is God denied.
— Sadhu Vaswani

I have a Friend. He protects me. He guards me in illness. He blesses me everyday. And He stretches forth His arms in love to enfold me in silence and darkness upon the night. He is your Friend, too. Indeed, He is the Friend of friends.
— Sadhu Vaswani

Where is God? How may we reach Him?

Significant are the words of the great German mystic and *brahmagyani*, Meister Eckhart, "Where creature stops, there God begins. All God wants of thee is to go out of thyself in respect of thy creatureliness and let God be the God-in-thee!"

Yes, all that is asked of us is to let go of our self— our petty selves of desire and passion and pride— and let God in. For He is our true self, our real self, the Self of our self.

All the time, while we are attending to our daily work, let our hearts be fixed on the true self within us, on God! Even as a ship moves hither and thither, but the needle of the compass of the ship is ever turned northward, even so let the ship of the body move hither and thither, attend to its multifarious duties, but let the needle of the heart's compass be ever directed towards God. This will happen through practice. Everything that we do, let it be done for the love of God. "For Thy sake, O Lord!" Let this be the one mantra of our life. Wondrous beyond words is the teaching of the Lord in the *Gita*, "O Arjuna! Whatever you eat, whatever you give in charity, whatever austerity you practise, whatever you do, do it all as an offering unto Me!"

Do we really need God in this day and age?

"If God did not exist, it would be necessary to invent Him," said Voltaire. The question arises, what sort of a God do we want? The vast majority of men and women want a God who is a sort of a store-keeper ready to supply them all those things for which they send in a requisition— the wealth of the world, its pleasures and power.

So long as God gives them what they want, He is good, kind, and loving. God is wise, and there is none like Him. But the moment He refuses to oblige, He becomes a cruel God, unjust and unkind. His very existence is denied.

The God of the majority of us is a "servant" God— ready to do our bidding, eager to satisfy our craving and caprices the moment they arise.

In plain words, we do not want to do God's Will. We want God to do our will. The more we strive for our will to be done, the more restless do we become, and consequently, the more unhappy and miserable. It is only God's Will that can restore harmony and order. Until I learn to submit to the Will of God, even if I reach out to the moon and conquer the stars, I shall but continue to wander from restlessness to restlessness.

What we need is not this, that or any other thing. What we require is a divine adjustment. At some time or the other, this truth dimly dawns on our consciousness. Pressed hard by circumstances, surrounded on all sides by trials and temptations, failure and frustrations, we feel like turning to God as the only remedy. But we are afraid to leave things in His hands for fear of what He may do.

How may we draw close to God?

He who stands still in the Lord finds everything in the Lord. The things he pursued and which eluded him, now come running to him. He desires them no longer. He seeks them no more. But they come to him of their own volition. He needs nothing. He has attained to the stage where he has neither hunger nor thirst.

They who are united with the Lord, are happy, indeed. Their wills are merged with the Will divine. They desire naught but what the Lord wills. They have broken the chains of bondage: They are attached to none: The Lord is their sheet anchor!

The one thing needful is to focus the mind on God, to live in His presence and to dedicate ourselves to Him.

Can we really understand God?

God is the goal of life. And God is to be realised, not merely "understood" or talked about. Long have we chanted hymns and recited from the scriptures and rung temple-bells and offered unending prayers, while our minds have strayed afar. Long have we kept God out of our lives. It is time to call Him in.

There is a beautiful picture by a great artist, Holman Hunt. In the picture, Christ is seen standing in a garden holding a lantern in one hand and with the other, knocking on a door. A friend of the artist said to him, "Holman, you have made a mistake. The door you have painted does not have a handle."

"It is not a mistake," answered the artist. "For that is the door of the human heart and can only be opened only from the inside!"

To move Godward, we need to get up and open the door and let God in. This happens only when man realises the need for God. Out of the very depths of his heart, there awakes the cry, "I have need of You, Lord! I cannot live without You!"

This is known as spiritual awakening. Something happens deep within you and your life becomes new. You are filled with light and warmth, joy and peace. You realise that the life you had lived until then— a life of creature comforts and of pride, pelf, power— was not life at all. You exclaim with Tolstoy, "To know God is to love!"

Dada, how may we live this new life in God? Please give us some practical suggestions?

1. The secret of the new life is love of God. This love grows from more to more. Love is a gift of God to man. Therefore, pray as

often as you can, "I love You, God! I want to love You more and more. I want to love You more than anything in the world. I want to love You to distraction, to intoxication. Grant me pure love and devotion for Thy Lotus Feet, and so bless me that this world-bewitching *maya* may not lead me astray. And make me, blessed Master, an instrument of Thy help and healing in this world of suffering and pain."

2.   There comes a stage when we realise that we cannot serve two masters at the same time. A decision has to be taken— either God or the world. We can't have both. There must be no compromise. The seeker after God stands up for truth— in thought, in speech, and in all his dealings with others. Truth— though she take me to gallows! Truth— though she lead me through the flames!

3.   If you have wronged a person, do not waste time in making amends. Have you hurt someone? Have you cheated him? Have you spread scandals against him? Have you exploited him for selfish purposes? Then waste no time in setting right what has gone wrong.

4.   Has someone wronged you? Forgive him even before forgiveness is asked. And your mind will be at peace and the world around you will smile.

5.   Whatever you do— it may be a lowly act such as sweeping a room or a noble deed such as saving a life— do it wholly for the love of God. "Whatever you eat, whatever you do, do it, O Arjuna, as an offering unto Me," says the Lord in the *Gita*. Can there be a simpler way of communing with God than this, that we offer unto Him every little thing we do, every thought we think, every word we utter, every aspiration we breathe?

6.   Establish more and more points of contact with God. This will give you soul-rest, and out of you the joy of God will flow to

many. Be gentle with all those who come to you. They have been sent by God to your door, not without a purpose.

7. Help as many as you can to lift the load on the rough road of life. Sadhu Vaswani said,

Did you meet him on the road?

Did you leave him with the load?

Dear Dada, how does God receive our messages?

God is the nearest of the near. He is the dearest of the dear. God is closer to us than breathing, nearer than hands and feet. God is not a far-off shadowy being, dwelling on a distant star. He is within every heart. Each one has a special God for himself as it were. You and God are inter-connected. The tiniest whisper of the human heart is audible to His ears. You do not have to speak to Him on the telephone. There is a hotline between Him and you all the time. You have barely given your message and it reaches Him. And He gives the answer. So many who meet me say to me, we have prayed and prayed and prayed but we don't receive any answer from God. I tell them, God gives us an answer immediately. Only we have to be receptive.

Dada, isn't it selfish to turn to God when we are in trouble?

Calling upon God for help in times of trial and tribulation may appear to some to be a very selfish act. But all our acts, in the beginning, have to be selfish, until we learn to become "spectators" and watch the drama of life unfold itself on the stage of time. If to rely upon God is to be selfish, it is far better to be "selfish" than to be "egoistic" and rely upon our own limited powers. This "selfishness" is a necessary step in our spiritual evolution and will, at the right time, drop of its own accord, even as the flower drops, when the fruit is born.

When will I be able to see God as I see others?

That depends on each individual. When the *antahkarana* the inner self, the inner instrument is purified, man sees God face to face. It was Jesus who said, "Blessed are the pure in heart for they shall see God." Until my heart has become completely pure, I cannot see God.

We asked Sadhu Vaswani, "You tell us God is everywhere. He is omnipresent. There is not a nook, a corner where He is not. Why is it that we are unable to see Him?"

Sadhu Vaswani said, "If a mirror is greased, can you see your face in it? You cannot. Similarly to see God, you need to purify the mirror of your heart." Therefore purify your heart. Cleanse it of all resentment, ill-will, jealousy, malice, hatred, lust, greed and anger. Through our daily thoughts, actions, words, we keep on adding stains to the mirror. Cleanse the mirror of your heart and you will behold the Beloved face to face.

How can I communicate with God?

You can communicate with God very easily—even as you are communicating with me! God listens to every word that you speak, every thought that you think.

Prayer is one way of communicating with Him. Meditation is another. He hears your softest whisper; He Himself speaks to you in silence. But very often we do not hear Him because we are lost in the noise and turmoil of this world. Within us is the clash of conflicting desires, and so we fail to hear the still, soft voice that sounds within us all the time. Be still, and look within you. Descend deeper and deeper within yourself, until you reach that still point where the white light shines—there you will hear His voice; there God will communicate with you and you will communicate with Him.

How may we experience the love of God?

This love is experienced when you are in the presence of the beloved. The simplest and easiest way to achieve it is through *sanga*, fellowship with those who love God. Love is not taught, it is caught. It is caught through contact with people who know what love is.

Prayer is also a great way to experience this love, for in prayer, we reach out to God.

Nishkam seva is another beautiful way that is open to us— selfless service of the poor and broken ones, in whom we may behold images of God. When I go out and serve a poor man, I am not doing him a favour; I am offering my little act of service at the Lotus Feet of the Lord in the hope that He will accept it. When I do that, my *antahkarna* or inner instrument is purified, and it is in the pure heart that love awakens.

My heart must be pure if it is to receive the gift of love.

How can we attain to God?

If you wish to attain to God, you must move in quest of Him. There are a number of ways that have been indicated to us for this purpose. In fact, there are as many ways to God, to the truth of life, as there are the souls of men. Each soul must tread its own path but the great ones have brought these paths together under certain categories, called *margas*.

One such *marga* is the way of self-enquiry. Find out who you are, what you are, why you have come to this earth plane. When you discover your true self, it will be easy for you to know God. Many of us are in contact with our lower self— the self of passion and pride, greed and egoism. We have to transcend this lower self and attain the higher self. This is the way of self-knowledge.

The second way is the way of selfless service. Go out and serve the broken, bleeding, suffering world, without expecting anything in return— not even a word of thanks. The ego must not enter this service; you must merely regard yourself as an instrument of that great cosmic power that is working through all of us.

The third way is the way of self-surrender. You surrender yourself to the higher power completely in a spirit of acceptance.

These are the three main paths indicated to us. Each one must follow the path that suits his temperament, or consult a spiritual elder who can show him the way.

What is the difference between deva, avatara and God?

God defined is God denied. We can say many things concerning what God is not. We cannot say what God is, because He is beyond the reach of the senses and the mind—beyond the reach of words.

The *avatara* is God made manifest. The literal meaning of *avatara* is "the descended one". The difference between the ordinary being and the *avatara* is that *karma* does not bind an *avatara*. We are bound by *karma*. As prisoners, we enter again and again, into the cycle of birth and death. To all appearances, the *avatara* is a man amongst men, but though men are bound by *karma*, he is ever free.

The literal meaning of the word *deva* is a "resplendent being", a "shining one". There is the world of *devas*, and each *deva* is assigned a specific duty in the government of the cosmos.

Buddhism is regarded as an atheist religion by some. It is said that the Buddha did not believe in God. What is your view?

Gautama Buddha did not reject God. During his time, many evil things were done in the Name of God and religion. The Buddha raised his voice against them.

In the days of the Buddha, it was believed that God could be actuated by malice, that God could be tempted and bribed and had favourites. The Buddha did not believe in such a God. His soul rose in rebellion against a God who required for his satisfaction the sacrifice of living creatures.

In the days of the Buddha many so called religious people took the Name of God and had debates over questions of speculative philosophy. The Buddha did not approve of this. To his disciples, he said, "Why do you waste your time over useless things? Your house is on fire. Go and quench the flames."

So whenever they asked him about God, the Buddha remained silent. Hence the impression that the Buddha did not believe in God. The Buddha understood that so much talk of God was useless. God, he felt, was to be realised, not talked about.

Why is it that God is not always with everyone?

God is always with everyone, but everyone is not always with God. During the days of the American Civil War, a woman said to Abraham Lincoln, "I am sure, God is on our side." Immediately Abraham Lincoln said, "What is more important is whether we are on the side of God." God is always with us, we are not always with God. The very fact that we carry the burdens of worry and anxiety on our tiny shoulders is testimony to the fact that we are not with God. Else, we would hand over all our burdens to God. Let me tell you a story.

A man of God and a barber once moved out together. As they passed by a slum area, the barber remarked, "Where is your God? Look at the misery that is around you. Tell me, where is your God?" The man of God remained silent.

Soon thereafter, they passed by a man with dishevelled hair and a half-shaven beard. Pointing to him, the holy man asked the barber,

"Where were you, my friend barber? Look at this man's hair and beard!"

"But he has never come to me!" was the answer of the barber.

And the holy man gently replied, "It is because so many people, the slum dwellers and others, have not come to God that their condition is so pitiable."

Of which God do you speak, Dada? Each religion has its own.

The rituals are different but the essential message of all the religions is the same. Religion has two aspects: the external and the internal. In the external aspect religions differ, but not so in their essential teachings. The God of all is love.

Man invented God at a time when he could not understand most of the natural phenomena. He felt insecure. But now, has he not reached a stage where he can do away with God?

Doing away with God is like doing away with life because God is the Life of our life. He is the Breath of our breath. He is the Universal Self, which is in each one of us. The concept of God itself has evolved. The anthropormorphic concept of God can be done away with but not God. How can I get away from my true Self?

Would you say that idol worship is a backward mode of worshipping God?

In India, we have spiritual food for every type of man— from the most primitive to the most evolved. Now the most primitive man sees his God in stone. When you evolve, you realise that God has no form at all. You can go beyond that too because God is beyond form and formlessness. He transcends all concepts.

Why did God create the world? Why did we get separated from Him when we were one with Him?

Similar questions were put to the Buddha. He said, "There was a man whose house had caught fire. The neighbours all rushed to his help. They said to him, you get out of this house, else you will get burnt to ashes. But the man said, "I will not leave this house until you tell me what caused the fire. Secondly, you tell me what is the temperature of the fire. Thirdly, you tell me what are the chemical constituents of the fire. Until I get an answer to these questions, I will not leave the house." Gautama said to the people around him, "Your house is burning; your house is on fire and you want answers to these questions? What you must do is first go and quench the flames! Get to the reality, to the higher self. Know what you are and all these questions will be answered." So I will tell you not to waste your time over these questions.

To these two questions that you have asked, there can be a hundred and one answers and there can be endless discussions.

The best thing is to get to God— God realisation. That is why the human body has been given to us. And when you come face to face with God, put to Him these questions. "God, why did You create the world? Why did we get separated from You when we were one with You?"

He is the only one who can give you the correct answer.

If I give you an answer, somebody else will give you another answer. A third person will give you yet another. Then there will be endless discussions. Get to God, and find out from Him.

To the second question, I would answer: In the beginning we were with God, but we wanted to have a taste of the rest of the world.

Concerning Parvati, we are told in the *Puranas*, that when she was married to Lord Shiva, she said to him, "Now that I have attained to you. I do not want anything else. I just want to be near you, that's all. Don't keep me away from yourself even for a single moment. Even if you are in meditation, permit me to sit by your side. I will keep on looking at you."

Parvati had to go through great *tapasyas*, to get to Shiva. Shiva was a *fakir*. He used to wear snakes round his neck. He was not the man to get entangled in marriage. So Parvati; through *taposhakti*, the power of *tapasya*, of austerity, attained to Shiva and said, "I have reached my goal, I want nothing else." Shiva smiled.

Many years elapsed. Parvati got used to Shiva. Once you get used to something all the glamour goes away. So after many years, many ages, Parvati said to Shiva,"I am here all the time on the peak of the Kailash mountain. It is so cold here. Let me go and see what is happening on earth. You have so many *bhaktas*, devotees. I would like to go and meet them."

Shiva said, "Remember the promise that you gave me?" But concerning women it is said, once they want a particular thing to happen, you cannot dissuade them from their resolve. They will be restless until they get it. Parvati would wait for a month or a two and again raise the topic until Shiva said, "All right, have your own way. You can go if you want to." She climbed down from the Kailash mountain.

There were so many *bhaktas*, so many devotees of the Lord. They were delighted that Parvati had come.

They had big *utsavas*, (functions) and Parvati said, "What was I doing all the time there on the Kailash mountain?

She was so happy. She moved from one place to another. Several years elapsed. Wherever she went, she was greeted by admiring crowds. She got so many gifts that she could not carry them and had to

cism. Violent Woman
cker Service Silence Spr powe
Gbrations Willpower Bhagavad
Of The World Selfishness Frustration Understand
Rituals Sadhu Vaswani Fear Forg
Thought Power Education Faith Meditation Min
And G

distribute them. Then she went to the South of India. There they have a temple built to commemorate this event.

When she got there, she began to have a longing again for Shiva. "So many years have passed," she said to herself, "I have been away from the beloved of my heart. But now, how can I get back to him?" She had lost the way. In all the adulation that she received, the admiration of the crowds, she had forgotten the way back.

She wept, shed tears at that spot and prayed, "Lord, I cannot reach You but You can reach me anywhere." Then it is said that the Lord came and took Parvati back and Parvati said, "I will never leave you again."

What is the goal of life?

Absorbed, as we are in the pursuit of the shadow-shapes of wealth and pleasure and power, we will do well to pause to ask ourselves the question, "What is the goal of life?" It cannot be wealth or possessions, pleasure or power, for we drop the body. What, then, is our life's goal? The goal is God!

There are some people who do not believe in God, but acknowledge that there is a supernatural power that is above us all. Do you think that such people are subconsciously aware of God's existence?

"God" is a word that we use to describe the great power above us, and by this word, we mean a variety of things. If you believe in a supernatural power, that is enough. I often say that everyone believes in prayer. There is not a soul living on this earth, who at one time or another, finding himself in a difficult situation, at a dead end, as it were, has not cried out, "I am unable to cope with this situation. Is there none to help me?" That is a prayer. It is an appeal to a Power over and above oneself. If you believe in such a prayer, it is enough.

You don't have to call that Power, God.

Sadly, the word "God" seems to be discredited today because there are so many people who talk of God— but do not live by the ideals of love, truth and compassion which that word signifies. This is why there are some who begin to question the very existence of God.

Why does God give so much suffering and poverty to some people, while He blesses others with material wealth and happiness.

This opens up another question. What is true happiness? Wherein lies true happiness? If you think it lies in material comforts you are mistaken. I know a few billionaires in the West and many of them tell me they are beset with problems. One of them even wrote to me that not a single day passes, when he does not think of committing suicide! I relate this only to show you that material comforts and possessions do not always bring you happiness.

There are countries which are regarded as among the richest countries in the world. Their citizens have the highest per capita income and the people enjoy a very high standard of living. It is in those countries that we have the highest percentage of suicides every year. Judge for yourself— material comforts, opulence, and wealth on the one hand— and suicides on the other. It is time we revised our thinking on material wealth and happiness.

Does God become old?

Like the sun, God is ever ancient but ever new. The sun is so ancient, it has been shining for ages and aeons together but everyday it is new. God, too, is ever ancient and ever new.

Dada, we talk so much of God: but who exactly is He?

In the ancient scriptures, we are told that in the beginning there was the One. The One bethought to Itself: "I am One: let Me be many." And the One trod the tracks of time, and the One entered the

If all decisions are made by God, should we just sit back and relax?

God makes no decisions. When God created man, He gave to man the very freedom that He kept for Himself. Man has a choice to use freedom in the right or wrong way. Freedom entails responsibility and your choice creates your *karma*. Remember, what I am today, is the result of the choices I made yesterday. What choices I make today, will determine what I will be tomorrow.

Guru

I offer myself in sacrifice to the Guru, a hundred times a day.
– Kabir

The Guru is the ladder, the dinghy,
the raft by means of which one reaches God;
The Guru is the lake, the ocean, the boat,
the sacred place of pilgrimage, the river.
Without the Guru, there can be no bhakti, no love.
– Guru Nanak

Is it true that one cannot reach God if he is not initiated by a perfect master?

There are some great ones who have reached God without any formal initiation. Lord Buddha is one such great soul, who was not initiated by a master, and yet he attained true enlightenment. There are others like him too.

The world is full of people who seek the Light, seek salvation, and are looking for the right Guru. How can we find our Guru, when people are calling so many men "Gurus"?

We cannot find our Guru. It is he who will come and find us. And when he does, you will feel, "This is my Guru! He is the one I have been waiting for all these years! My blessed master, why were you away from me for so long?" He, in his grace will find you.

Even if we try to find our Guru on our own, we are likely to be misled, for the world is full of deceptions, and we may be led astray. The Guru may even come to you in your thoughts and dreams. The Guru exists at a higher level, while we exist on a lower level. So it is he who must find us.

Can a Guru change our destiny?

Why should he? The true Guru will always say, "Accept it." Yes, the Guru will do everything for his disciple to help him grow spiritually. Why should a Guru interfere with the Will of God? The Guru can provide the disciple with a buffer to enable him to bear the shocks of life without breaking down. It is very much like the surgeon administering anesthesia to his patient before performing the operation. The patient goes through the process without feeling the pain, which might otherwise have killed him.

h Disci
Liberation Life Lov
Egoism Violent Dreams
Seeker Service Silence Spirituality
Vibrations Willpower Woman Yoga Any
Of The World Bhagavad Gita God
Selfishness Frustration Worry
Rituals Sadhu Vaswani Science An
Thought-Power Understanding
Education Faith Fear
Meditatio

In the olden days, people used to go to holy men. Nowadays it is the holy men who go to the people, wherever they may be around the world. What is the rationale behind this?

There was a time when people regarded going to holy men as part of their duty. The *purusharthas* placed before them were four:

Artha—economics.

Kama—the pleasure principle.

Dharma—righteousness.

Moksha—liberation.

Every man felt it was his duty to work for *moksha*. So people went to holy men. Today people have forgotten this, they are lost in the lore of less and more. They don't think of *moksha*. Therefore, perhaps, the holy ones think it their duty to go to the people.

As it seems, many so-called Gurus take advantage of this. There are many Gurus, who do not dwell in the light. Nor does the light dwell in them. Today, if a person has the gift of the gab, he can easily become a Guru. All the more reason why the holy ones— those who are true Gurus— deem it their duty to awaken humanity.

We are aware that sometimes the Guru takes on the karmas of the disciple. Can the disciple share the burden of the Guru? If yes, how?

He can, if he is strong enough. He has to develop spiritual strength before he can share the Guru's burden. In fact it is the duty of every disciple to share the burden of the Guru. But where are they who can share the burden? They will get crushed unless they have developed that spiritual strength that will enable them to share it. So the very first thing is to develop spiritual strength. Even as we develop our muscular strength with the help of dumb-bells and other equipment, even so must we develop our spiritual muscles. Once you are spiritually strong, you can share the burdens of the Guru.

Sant Eknath was a disciple of Janardhan Swami. Janardhan Swami was the governor, in charge of a fort. Once a week, Janardhan Swami devoted the whole day to silence, meditation and communion. Taking advantage of this, a Muslim king invaded the fort on the day of Janardhan's weekly retreat.

The Muslim ruler was sure that victory would be his, for nothing would distract the governor from his prayer and meditation. At that time, Sant Eknath was only a boy of sixteen or seventeen years. Sensing that the enemy would conquer the fort if no quick action was taken, this young boy entered the Guru's room, put on the Guru's armour, took the Guru's horse and led the Guru's army onwards. He won the battle, routed the enemy and returned to the fort.

Quietly, he stabled the horse, returned the armour to the Guru's room, and attended the evening prayer meeting of the Guru, without uttering a word about his actions.

After some days, Janardhan Swami came to know of the incident and was wonder struck!

It is only when you develop spiritual strength that you are ready to shoulder the burdens of the Guru.

Is a Guru necessary for developing spiritual strength and, if so, how do we discern the Guru who is a wolf in sheep's clothing?

A Guru becomes necessary only when you feel that he is necessary, not otherwise. A stage comes in the life of every spiritual aspirant when he realises the need for a Guru— someone who can hold him by the hand and take him onward, forward, upward, inward,

Liberation Life Death Dreams Spirituality
sion, Egoism, Violent Dreams Silence Spirituality Yoga Worry Science Sin
Seeker Service Silence Willpower Woman Yoga Bhagavad Gita Frustration Worry Understanding
Vibrations Of The World Selfishness, Frustration Thought-Power Education Faith Fc
Rituals Sadhu Vaswani Science Meditat

Godward. When he feels that need, it is only then that he should aspire for a Guru. Pray to the Lord, "Lord, put me into contact with someone, a man of Light, with someone who can connect me with You, with someone who has known You, and knows the Way."

Then sheep's clothing or lion's clothing will not matter at all. You don't go out in quest of the Guru. The Guru will come to you himself. You will see him and you will realise that he is the person meant for you. If you go out in quest of the Guru, you will be disillusioned. There are so many who are not real Gurus, who are not men and women of attainment but who pretend that they are. So, aspire. This is the law of spiritual life— whatever you aspire for, will come to you. Only, that aspiration, that longing, that yearning of the heart should be strong and deep. Then yearning takes the form of a cloud and when the cloud becomes heavy enough, it starts to pour and out of the cloud, will come your Guru.

It is not impossible to reach the Highest without any outside help. But for most of us, if we wish to learn anything, we need a teacher. If we want to learn geography, we have to go to a teacher. Why, if I want to learn how to steal, I must make a thief my teacher. Otherwise I won't be able to learn stealing. That is why they have schools for pick pockets! For spiritual progress, too, which is the most important thing in life surely, many of us need a teacher.

Dadaji, I would like to know, how can one recognise a true master?

Can a little child know who is a good teacher? When the little child comes to the school, he will not know who is a good teacher. It will be difficult for those who are on a lower level to decide about those at a higher level. But there are certain marks by which we can get an indication.

zcism, Violent Silence Spirit
eeker Service Silence Spiri
Vibrations Willpower Woman
Of The World Bhagavad Gi
Selfishness, Frustration, W
Rituals Sadhu Vaswani Sci
Thought-Power Understanding
Education Faith Fear Forg
Meditation M
And C

The true master will not want anything for himself. He will not ask for anything. He has come to the earth only to give. Sadhu Vaswani used to say, today's Gurus have become *ghurus*. *Ghuru* means takers.

A true Guru has transcended the ego. It does not exist in him. He is humble, childlike, innocent, and pure.

A true Guru lives in the light and the light lives in him. The literal meaning of the word Guru is *"gu" "ru"*. *Gu* is darkness, *ru* is light. Guru is the one who leads us out of darkness into light.

The true master does not call himself a master. The true Guru does not call himself a Guru. He says, "I am a disciple like any one of you."

Very close to Delhi is a station called Nizamuddin, named after a great Sufi master, Hazrat Nizamuddin. He used to say, "It is the privilege of the disciple to decide who will be, his Guru. It is not the privilege of the Guru to decide who will be his disciple."

There are Gurus, today, who will suddenly catch hold of you and tell you that you are my disciple. But that is not the correct thing. No Guru wishes to increase the number of his disciples. The Guru rather wishes to decrease the number of his so-called disciples.

The Guru says, let every disciple come upto a stage where he is no longer a disciple. He becomes a master himself. If a disciple becomes a master, the number of the Guru's disciples decreases.

Is it necessary to get Naam from your spiritual master? Please explain.

That depends upon the master. Some of the greatest spiritual masters in the world don't believe in giving a particular *Naam*. They will just tell you that all Names will lead you to God. Choose the Name that appeals to you and repeat it.

Dadu, who is regarded as one of the world's greatest mystics has sung many *dohas*. In one of his *dohas* he says, "*Dadu sirjan- har ke kete Naam anant, chit aavey so leejeye, yeh sadhu simran sant.*" He says, "God, the Creator of the universe, has a myriad Names. Whatever Name appeals to you, whatever Name you can repeat with love in your heart, choose that Name and repeat it."

I saw a woman turning rosary beads and reciting the sacred mantra, "*Hare Rama, Hare Rama*". Suddenly, she exclaimed to her servant, "Boy, have you kept the pot on the fire?" Then again she started, "*Hare Rama, Hare Rama*". "Boy, have you put the proper quantity of salt in the vegetable?" Then again, "*Hare Rama, Hare Rama*". That is not the right way of repeating the Name. It is worse than useless. It is worse than being a tape recorder. In no case does the tape recorder pause and ask, "What have you kept on the fire? Has the salt been added and so on."

Whatever be the Name of God you choose, you should repeat it with deep feeling and emotion. There are some masters who will ask you to repeat a particular Name. There are others like Sri Ramana Maharishi, Sri Ramakrishna Paramahansa, who didn't believe in doing this.

When a person has chosen a spiritual path, it is very difficult to know what type of activities he or she should be involved in. Would you kindly give me some suggestions on how to differentiate between the do's and don'ts in life because I do not wish to do anything that my Guru wouldn't like.

I think once you have set foot on the spiritual path, all you are required to do is to beware of the ego.

The spiritual path is the path of annihilation of the ego. It is not what you do that matters, it is the way you do it. If your actions inflate your ego, refrain from doing them. If it deflates your ego, you are on the right path.

Never do a thing which inflates your ego. If there is one thing that stands between you and your Guru, between us and God, it is the ego.

It is like this. The sun is shining. Suppose we cover our eyes with the palm of our hand, the sun will not be seen by us. The sun is 91 times bigger than the earth, but it can be hidden with the palm of our hand. Similarly, the ego is very small. But because we magnify it in our daily life beyond all proportion, it has come and taken hold of us.

I am told that one should not be attached to the Guru. In other words, one has to go beyond the desire to be physically near him. Please throw some light on this.

You have to go beyond that, but I think this is a necessary stage that you should, in the beginning, be attached to the form of a Guru. In fact, the Guru himself draws you, so that you are liberated from attachment to worldly forms. Afterwards, when you are attached to the Guru, the Guru detaches himself. It is up to the Guru to do it. But in the beginning we should feel drawn to the Guru. The vibrations that emanate from him should draw us.

Once he withdraws himself, we cry out for him. Sometimes, we even call him a tyrant. But he does all this to annihilate our ego. Guru is *Brahma*, Guru is *Vishnu*, and Guru is *Maheshwara*. So the work of *Maheshwara* is to destroy. Destroy what? The ego of the disciple.

Give some simple practical instructions which we may follow in our daily life to displace the ego from its position of sovereignty and unlimited power.

Here are a few simple suggestions:

1. When in the midst of friends or strangers, refrain from pushing yourself forward. See how at the slightest excuse you try to show yourself off.

2. Refrain from much talk. The less you talk, the less you will be noticed and the more you will be permitted to recede in the background. As it is, we talk too much. In fact, we always try to monopolise conversation. It was only this morning that a friend came to you and tried to speak to you of the burden on his mind. He had scarcely begun, when you cut him short and delivered to him a discourse on accepting the Will of God. Can you truthfully say that in every situation of life, you accept the Will of God? Then, what right have you to lecture others? It will do you immense good if you remain silent and let others talk.

3. What helps is not your words but your vibrations. What transforms is not your lectures but your silent prayers. So talk little to those whom you wish to help, but pray for them, again and again.

4. Always keep clear of the desire of telling others of your life and achievements, your inner struggles and experiences, your opinions and aspirations. Live and grow in the thought that you are a tiny particle of dust and that no one cares for what you think or say, nor misses you when you are away.

5. Your real value lies not in your outer, empirical self but in your inner, imperishable self: and this inner self cares not for the applause of others. It is firmly established in itself.

6. Cultivate friendship with this inner self. And meditate on the significant words of the *Gita*:

He who hath conquered

His lower self of cravings and desires,

He hath his supreme friend found

In the self, immortal, true!

But he who's still a victim

To his appetites and passions,

Verily, the self becometh to him

Hostile as an enemy!

Practise these six precepts for a week and notice the change that comes upon you!

Why do two messengers of God contradict one another when a similar question is put to them?

I don't think it's true. I think the contradiction is in our own minds and not in the answers. We do not understand the two answers properly.

There was a young man. He fell in love with a girl. He went to a holy woman. She said to him, "Don't worry my boy, you will get what you want. But now is the time for you to study." Later he went to a holy man. He told him, "This is not the age for you to be running after girls. You must apply your mind to your studies and show brilliant results. When the time comes, if it be God's Will, you will get the girl." This young man said, "Why this contradiction?"

Actually there is no contradiction. If you go into the depths, there is no contradiction. By the time you grow up, perhaps you don't want the girl at all. I know of boys madly in love with girls. But when they grow up they say, "Please don't show us her face." These things have happened.

The other day, I was telling my *satsangi* brothers and sisters an incident of a young man who wanted to marry a girl. For eighteen years he kept on chasing her. Finally he was married to her and felt that his dream was fulfilled. He met me only a week after his marriage and told me, "I am living in hell. When will I be free from the girl?"

So you don't know what you are asking for. Maybe what you are asking for is poison. And God does not wish to give you poison.

I know of a child, three years old, who was the only child of the family. The father was a very wealthy man and said to the little boy, "Everything belongs to you. Whatever you want, you can have." One day, the boy found his father shaving and asked for a blade. "I will not give you the blade," the father said. The boy was disillusioned. This boy of three years said, "Only the other day daddy said everything belongs to me. I asked for a single blade and I am denied having it."

From the point of view of the child, it was alright. But the father would not give a blade to a three-year old, lest he cut his own finger. We do not know what is for our own good.

The teachings of the holy ones are the same. The contradiction is in our minds. We have, therefore, to try and understand the teachings of the holy ones not merely with the help of the mind. We must go beyond the mind. The *Gita* says, beyond the five senses— eyes, ears, nose, tongue, and touch, is the mind. But beyond the mind is the *buddhi*. Some call it intellect. Some call it the higher reason, the higher intellect.

We should try to understand with the higher intellect and not with the mind. The mind will not be able to give you the correct interpretation of the teachings of the great ones.

Tell us something about your Guru?

My revered *Gurudeva*, Sadhu Vaswani, was a picture of love. The treasure of my life, he said, is love. Love flowed out of him in an endless, ceaseless stream. It drew many of us, unworthy souls, nearer to his lotus-feet. In our hearts, we adored him as our Guru. But he refused to be called a Guru. "I am a Guru of none," he said. "I am a disciple of all!" His humility was so touching! He would not permit us to touch his feet. Before we could bow low to take the sacred dust of his feet, his hands were already on our feet! It was only at night, when he went to sleep, that I had an opportunity of kissing his holy feet.

What are the essential marks of a true Guru?

The marks of a true Guru are many. He is, essentially, a man of light. He dwells in the light and the light dwells within him. We are in the darkness of *avidya*, ignorance, duality. The Guru takes us out of this darkness into the light of the One-in-all, the One that is all. That is something only the Guru can do.

The Guru is a man of many qualities. He is free from sensuality: in him there is no drag of the flesh. He is a picture of purity. He is free from greed. He has no desire for wealth or worldly possessions. He does not seek earthly greatness: he does not even desire that his following should increase. In his heart, there is no feeling of hatred or enmity towards anyone. He has conquered the weaknesses of the flesh and the mind. He has, specially, these three marks, love, humility and wisdom.

Sadhu Vaswani was such a one. His love drew us as a magnet draws a needle. No one could resist the power of his love which flowed alike to the saint and the sinner, the friend and the foe. His humility defied description. It was the humility of one who had reduced himself to nought. "*Naham! Naham! Tuho! Tuho!*" He said, again and again. "I am nothing! Thou alone art, O Lord!" In his life, he revealed what it was to become nothing, no-thing. And as Jesus said, "The empty alone are filled." Beloved Sadhu Vaswani became empty of the self, the ego and the Lord filled him with love and wisdom. He had the wisdom of the truly wise, of those who had touched the root of life and unravelled the secrets of the Spirit. So it is, that he could express the most profound truths in a language so simple that even a child could understand.

There is something which only the Guru can do. How does he go about doing it? Is there anything that the Guru gives to the disciple?

There is nothing that the Guru has to give us. For, everything is within us already. God himself is within everyone! What hides God from us is our little "ego". When it goes, God's light glows! And it is the constant endeavour of the Guru to destroy our "ego" which, in reality, has no existence, but is a mere shadow. The Guru draws us to himself through the irresistible power of his love— and then weans us from the "ego". He takes up the *trishul* (the trident) and strikes the "ego". In the process, the disciple may have to undergo great mental torture. Blessed is he who does not resist and says, "My body and my mind, all that I have and I am, I offer unto thee! Do with me what thou wilt!"

Yogi Mahadev did not have disciples. One day, a young man came to him asking to be accepted as a disciple. The *yogi* said to him, "I will accept you on one condition. Go to yonder point where the mountain ends and jump down from the precipice." The young man was flabbergasted. "If I do that," he said, "I shall die!" The *yogi* smiled as he said, "Unless you die, how can you be re-born?" The young man asked, "If I die, who will become the disciple?" The *yogi* answered, "It is only when you die that you can receive the gift of the new life." "How is that?" asked the young man. And the *yogi* said, "You are a farmer. You know very well that until the grains of wheat die in the earth, they cannot yield a new crop." The young man nodded and went away.

Can you suggest some ways to overcome the nervousness, or the fear of confession?

I think one thing that helps is this. If I cannot confess to the Guru in person, let me take the Guru's picture in a closed room and confess to the picture. Let me blurt out all and as I do so, gradually I will find it easier to confess to the Guru. But let it come out audibly, vocally in words, not just in the heart. To start with, we can take up the picture of our *Ishtadeva* e.g. Krishna, Rama, Jesus, Buddha, Zoroaster, Baha'u'llah. We first confess to the *Ishtadeva*. Just sit in front of the picture, feel His presence, and tell Him, "This is my difficulty, this is what I have been doing. I need Your grace, I need Your strength, Your wisdom and Your purity. Without it, I am nowhere. I am helpless, and there are forces that drag me in that direction. Now, You must stand by me." That will help. Then gradually that lower self will be so trained that it will not object if you go and talk to the Guru and confess to him.

One very good discipline in spiritual life is, everyday, preferably at the same time, at the same place, go and sit in silence and think of all the things that you did during the earlier twenty four hours. But begin with what you did now, then what you did a minute earlier. Then go in the backward direction. You will find that there were many things that you should have done and did not do, as there were many things that you did, which you should not have done— acts of omission and commission. Then ask for the strength not to repeat those mistakes. Repeat this exercise day after day. You will find that within six months, your life will change considerably. But do it everyday as a *sadhana*, a spiritual discipline.

If one has chosen a Guru for whom he has no shraddha (faith), can one turn to a second Guru?

The first thing you must understand is that there is one Guru seated in the hearts of all of us. He is the *Satguru*, the Master, God Himself! A Guru, in physical form, shows us the way to the *Satguru*, and under certain conditions, takes us along to meet Him too. But to attain this goal, it is absolutely essential to have *shraddha* in the Guru we have chosen.

Whatever worldly art or craft we wish to learn, we cannot learn properly unless we have faith in our teacher. Without faith, we can learn nothing. Without *shraddha*, the Guru can give us nothing— and the loss is not his, but ours.

Can we have more than one Guru? Let me put it this way. Suppose I have chosen someone as my Guru, when that Guru has fulfilled his part, then the *Satguru* who is seated in my heart, leads me on to another Guru. The second Guru picks up the work where the first one has left off— it is like moving from one class to another in school.

Of *Dattatreya*, it is said that he had twenty four Gurus! Therefore, we can have more than one Guru. But whoever may be the Guru you choose, you must have *shraddha* in him— and never forget that the *Satguru* is seated in our heart, leading us through different experiences and preparing us for the final goal.

How can we gain our Guru's blessings?

By living our life in accordance with the teachings of the Guru, we can gain the Guru's blessings. No true Guru expects money, mere words or material gifts from his disciples. What he expects is the gift of life. Follow the teachings of the Guru in daily life. This is what makes him happy.

What also makes the Guru happy is when the number of his disciples is reduced. That is, when the disciple ascends to the level of the Guru and becomes a reflection of the Guru, this makes, the Guru happy.

Another thing that makes the Guru happy is when you bring aspiring souls— souls in whom there is the longing to live the true life—closer to him.

What is the difference between the words, sadhu and sant, Guru and Satguru?

Sadhu literally means "God man" and *sant* means "one who has reached the *ant*— the Ultimate— of life. *Satguru* is, the one who is seated in the heart. The *Satguru*, because He is invisible, takes on some form or the other and appears in the form of the *Guru*.

Health

The first wealth is health
— Emerson

Health is not a condition of matter, but of mind
— Mary Baker Eddy

Refuse to be ill. Never tell people you are ill; never own it to yourself.
Illness is one of those things which a man should resist on principle at the
onset.
— Bulwer Lytton

There's lots of people who spend so much time watching their health, they
haven't got time to enjoy it
— Josh Billings

What are your views on modern medicine?

The skills of modern medicine are amazing. The miracles of healing performed by modern medicine are astounding. But the time has come when modern medicine must take a step forward. Doctors must find a way of treating the whole man. Modern medicine takes care only of the body like a machine which can be repaired when it goes out of order. Man is a composite being built up of body, mind and soul. Each one of us is essentially a soul. If the soul be sick, do whatever you will to the body, it will keep on moving from one sickness to another. We need to treat the whole man.

Can positive attitudes influence our health?

Of course, yes! Always be positive in your outlook upon life and expect the best. Plant beautiful thoughts in your mind. Control your anger, and animal appetites. Many doctors are drawing a corelation between an individual's personality and the nature of his disease.

In a paper recently published in America, it has been shown that malignancy is caused by a great tendency to hold resentment and a marked inability to forgive. Give and forgive and live a healthy life!

Is health education necessary?

Dispensaries and hospitals are good and necessary. But what is more important is to spread health education among young adults and students. Life, today has become artificial. People have forgotten the laws of health and rely more and more on antibiotics, injections and drugs. We are all created to be healthy. And we can weaken our systems by our choices and our attitudes towards life and actually make ourselves ill. Today doctors are beginning to realise that it is more important to heal on the psychological and spiritual levels than on the physical.

Dada, can you give us the secrets of good health?

1. The foundation of a healthy body is a happy mind. Therefore,

let nothing agitate you or disturb your inner peace. Let the motto of your life be:

Thou knowest everything, beloved,

Let Thy Will always be done!

In joy and sorrow, my beloved,

Let Thy Will always be done!

There is a doctor who says to his patients, "Keep your upstairs (brain) clean and your downstairs (body) will be healthy!"

2. Eat a balanced diet.

3. Drink sufficient water (never alcohol).

4. Take plenty of fresh air and sunshine.

5. Laugh heartily. Laughter is at once a physical, mental and spiritual tonic. If possible, you must laugh heartily three times a day— before taking breakfast, lunch, dinner. But be careful not to laugh at others. Laugh with others and, if you can, laugh at yourself.

6. You must have sufficient sleep.

7. You must have adequate exercise. Walking is the king of exercises.

8. You must have proper elimination (via bowels, kidneys, lungs and skin).

9. Everyday you must spend some time in silence. Pray, meditate, repeat the Name Divine, engage yourself in a loving and intimate conversation with God, do your spiritual thinking.

You must adopt a cheerful and positive attitude. And you must always keep away from wrong habits such as smoking, drinking, drugs. Many promising lives have been sacrificed on the altar of wrong habits.

Hinduism

The Sanathana Dharma, the Eternal Religion declared by the Rishis, will alone endure.
– Sri Ramakrishna Paramahansa

Dada, tell us something about Hinduism.

Among all the great religions of the world, Hinduism occupies a unique position. It is the only religion that has not been founded by a person or persons. It has existed eternally without a founder. It does not rest on any beliefs or dogmas or on the words of a Prophet but on universal and eternal spiritual principles. Unlike other religions, which are organised institutions, Hinduism is not an organised religion but a self-evolved one. Other religions have their protectors and propangandists. Hinduism is scientific in its approach and is based on the reasoning and realisations (in super-conscious states) of great spiritual geniuses called *rishis*. Some of them like Sri Krishna— the Singer of the *Bhagavad Gita*, the song celestial, and Buddha and Shankaracharya and Sri Chaitanya Mahaprabhu, are considered as divine incarnations. Sri Krishna is considered to be God Himself who, wearing a human form, visited the earth to give salvation to millions. Jesus said, "I am the way and I am the goal!" and "Come unto Me, ye that are weary and heavy-laden and I shall give you rest." And Krishna said, "Renouncing all rites and writ duties, come to Me for single refuge, and I shall liberate you from all bondage to suffering and sin. Of this have no doubt."

What is the origin of Hinduism ?

Hinduism has no book, no founder, and no date of establishment. Its original name is *sanatana* dharma, which means the eternal religion. Of this eternal religion, all others are tributaries. Therefore, this tradition has no quarrel with other religions. *Sanatana* dharma has come to be known as Hindu *dharma*. But, this is not the original name. Hinduism says that you must respect every religion and not quarrel with any religion. It believes that there is truth in every religion.

*ation Life... Violent Dream... Spirituality... Yoga... Worry... Science...
-gcism... Service Silence Spirituality... Woman Yoga... Worry Science...
Seeker Vibrations Willpower Of The World Bhagavad Gita... Frustration... Sadhu Vaswani... Thought-Power... Understanding...
Selfishness, Frustration... Rituals Sadhu Vaswani... Education Faith Fear Fore...
Thought-Power... Education Faith Fear... Meditation M... And*

How is Hinduism different from other religions?

Hinduism has never been sectarian or bound by any creed or dogma and has a place for everyone. You may be an agnostic, even an atheist, and yet be a Hindu. For Hinduism gives the utmost freedom to the individual to think in his own way and regulate his life.

The Hindu seers believed that atheism, too, was a step in the spiritual advancement of a man. Swami Vivekananda said, "From the high spiritual flights of the *Vedanta* philosophy, of which the latest discoveries of science seem like echoes, to the low ideas of idolatory with its multifarious mythology, the agnosticism of the Buddhists and the atheism of the Jains, each and all have a place in the Hindu religion."

In some religions you are taught that if you do not believe in a particular creed, God, who all the time sits in judgement over you will punish you. In Hinduism, we are taught not to be afraid of God but to think of Him as an all-loving Father— or Mother— whom you may approach without any hesitation, at any time and in any place. The Hindu has a personal relationship with God— as a father, mother, brother, friend or the beloved. There are Hindu women who even regard God as their child.

In Hinduism, you are given complete freedom to think for yourself— not to accept anything on authority or hearsay, but to verify the truth of what is told to you before you accept it. You are not called upon to believe in a creed or dogma like the one that says that someone died for you to cleanse you of all your sins, or a similar thing, which you cannot verify. In Hinduism you are asked to do what you consider to be true. There is no place for sophistry and dogmatic fiat, or superstition and baseless beliefs. Man is given the freedom to investigate into the validity of the beliefs placed before him. It is no sin to doubt the very existence of God. Therefore, as has been said before, nihilism, atheism, agnosticism have their due place in one's sincere search for truth. Freedom is the first condition of growth— physical, mental, moral, spiritual.

Hinduism has given me the freedom to say: If Krishna is my father, Jesus and other great ones are my uncles.

What has been the attitude of non-Hindu religions towards Hinduism?

I read somewhere that the Hindus in Holland were not permitted to use the *havan kund* for worship or to immerse the last remains of their dead in the rivers, on the grounds that they might cause fire or pollution of the waters. Hindus have not been permitted to build temples and are forced to conduct their ceremonies in homes or hired halls. If discovered, the Hindus who participated at the ceremonies are arrested or heavily fined and the *havan kund* thrown out by the police.

Compare the freedom and facilities that the Hindus have extended to non-Hindu religions. Hinduism has always been eclectic— choosing the best out of other systems and absorbing it. This is what has made Hinduism a growing religion— a religion which, like the sun, is ever ancient, ever new.

What should be our attitude to different religions?

All great religions are equally true and equally imperfect. The different religions are like the branches of a tree; the tree of religion. The branches are all growing and the person who belongs to one growing branch cannot gloat over it and exclaim, "Mine is the superior branch: mine is the higher branch!"

There is no superior and there is no inferior. In the Kingdom of God, no one considers himself to be higher than the others. It was *ion Life* *Violent Dream* *Spirituality* *Woman Yoga* *Worry* *Science* *cism, Service Silence Spirituality* *Willpower Woman Yoga Bhagavad Gita* *Understanding* *eker Service Silence* *Of The World Bhagavad Gita Selfishness, Frustration Sadhu Vaswani Science* *Education Faith Fear Forgi* *spirations Willpower Woman* *Selfishness, Rituals Sadhu Thought Power Education Faith Meditation Min* *And Th*

Jesus who said, "He that would be the greatest amongst you, let him be a servant of all!"

To be a servant is not to convert, but to help each other to grow in the new life— the life of a new awakening, self-effacement and self-realisation.

Therefore, I must not criticise the religious beliefs of others which I cannot understand, but should express admiration for those aspects which I am able to appreciate and understand.

To be able to appreciate and understand other religions, I must see them through the eyes of the adherents of those religions. As a Hindu, it is my right and duty to point out the errors that have crept into Hinduism, so that it may grow in purity. When non-Hindu critics set about criticising Hinduism and prepare a catalogue of its faults and defects, they only reveal their own ignorance of the real teachings of their great ones and their great incapacity to regard Hinduism from the Hindu viewpoint. It distorts their vision and vitiates their judgement. It adds evil to the world. And it was Jesus who said, "Out of evil cometh good, but woe unto him who doeth the evil!"

Can I declare myself a Hindu, even if I belong to a different religion?

An American sister met me in Key West (USA) and said that after reading the *Bhagavad*, she was captivated by Krishna and so wanted to declare herself a Hindu. I said to her, "You must never do that. What the *Bhagavad* offers, the Bible also offers. You must make an attempt to find it out and be a good Christian. Every good follower of Christ is a good follower of Sri Krishna and other great ones of humanity. You will not draw closer to the heart of Krishna just by labelling yourself a Hindu. A Christian can be as dear to Sri Krishna as a Hindu. In the Kingdom of God there are no labels."

If a person wants to believe in Jesus and build his life in the great teachings of the Bible, let him do so, but why should he, on that account, discard his own religion, his own mother? Religion is a personal matter, the relationship of an individual with God. And God has many forms as God is without form. Truly, God is above both form and formlessness.

What is your advice to the youth of the Hindu faith?

Young men and women of the Hindu faith! Never forget that the blood of Hindu *rishis* and sages and saints courses through your veins. You belong to a religion, which is the hope of the world that is madly rushing from danger to destruction. Be proud of the fact that you are a Hindu! And in humility move out to share the treasures that are your rich heritage as children of the *rishis*.

Do not proselytise! Do not convert! But through the quiet, gentle, loving influence of your life, help your Christian friends to be better Christians, your Muslim friends to be better Muslims, your Jewish friends to be better Jews! And let every day of your life on earth be a search for the better, for that spiritual perfection which puts aside mountains and builds bridges of brotherhood over rivers and seas, so that you can meet your fellow men not with a grenade but with a warm, loving heart.

India

The soil of India is my highest heaven,
the good of India is my good.
– Swami Vivekananda

Why is it that even though so many Gurus and rishis and saints have been born in India, there is so much of suffering in the country?

It is because of the *rishis* and *Gurus* and saints that the people have the strength to accept everything with a smile. They believe that suffering comes not without a purpose. It is not something to be shunned.

The emphasis in the teachings of the great spiritual leaders of India is not on the outer things of life, the glamour and greatness of the world, but in unfolding the inner powers, the *atma-shakti*. It is because of this, *atma shakti*, the inner soul power, that India has been able to ride many a storm and quell many a tempest of time and history. When all other ancient civilisations have perished, India alone lives on! India lives to give this great message to the nations of the world that true freedom is not in outer things. There can be no freedom without spirituality.

Why do we Indians imitate the West when we have such a rich heritage of philosophy, culture and spiritualism? The Western philosophers, thinkers, who come to India in search of a philosophy, are surprised at our imitation of the Western society, which is decadent and crumbling.

For over ten centuries, India has lived in subjugation. Little wonder that, as a nation, we suffer from inferiority complex. The external glamour and affluence of Western nations easily dupes us: and we feel happy imitating them. All imitation and emasculation, is weakness.

As India grows in strength, she will press forward to a new dynamic march of her eternal genius, her own destiny. India has a mission to fulfil in the coming days. She has to reveal to the nations that there can be no true freedom without spirituality. India has much to learn of the West and vice versa. When the Indians learn to absorb the best in the life of the West and share with the Western nations the truths of her ancient culture, she will shine once again in the splendour of the new morning sun and will be respected as a leader of the nations and a builder of a new civilisation of simplicity and strength, brotherliness and fellowship, sympathy and service.

Dada, how is it that you still continue to have an optimistic picture of India?

The intellectualism and scientific explorations of Europe have been infected with calculated self-interest and narrow nationalism. India, among the nations of the earth, still has a vision of the *atman*, the one universal self in all, still believes in *daridra narayan* (the divine spirit in the poor), still adores God's vision in all races and religions, in all scriptures and sages. India holds the key to the future of the world. For India still thrills to the message of love and brotherhood, "He that loves not, lives not, and he that beholdeth the One-in-all and the All-in-one— he hath eternal life!"

Sadhu Vaswani was a voice of unity. He was an apostle of harmony, of renunciation and peace. He was a prophet of new India. The dream haunted him— the dream of an India of the truly strong and free— an India which would go out upon her mission of help and healing to the nations of the East and the West. He asked the young to strive after the ideal of sacrifice, not ambition; to be simple; to cooperate with all and not let differences in creed or political opinion stand in the way of solidarity; to help in reconstruction of village-life; and to accept the creative ideal which regards humanity as one and service as the end of all knowledge.

Sadhu Vaswani's message to the people was, "Unite and build". He urged that the one piteous need of India was unity. It's salvation lay in unity. Without India, he said, where would the world be? And without unity where would India be? "It is the duty of every Indian to bear witness, in deeds of daily living, to the great ideals of India's sages and saints. Through the example of his life, he must awaken the love of God and the spirit of service of the poor and lowly in the hearts of those around him."

What is the essence of India's culture?

The essence of India's culture is the vision of the One-in-all. India's greatest message to the nations is that life is one. The same life that is in you, is in me. We are not apart from one another. Electricity may flow through a bulb of 5-watts or 500-watts, but the electricity is the same. A 5-watt bulb will give you a little light and the 500-watt bulb will give you a blaze of light, but the power, the *shakti*, the light element that passes through both is the same.

Out of this vision of the One-in-all grows the spirit of reverence for all life. There are three kinds of reverence— reverence for what is above us, around us, and beneath us. By reverence for what is around us and above us, we mean reverence for God, and our spiritual elders, senior citizens, our friends, and our compatriots. Reverence for what is beneath us includes reverence for the poor, the broken ones, the handicapped, birds, and animals.

There is a unity of life. Creation is one family. In this one family of creation, birds and animals are man's younger brothers and sisters. That is India's culture. Dances and other elements of culture have grown out of this vision of the One-in-all. For instance, all music is harmony which grows out of the understanding of the One-in-all. If there is One-in-all, we must harmonise with all.

Karma

The arm of the moral universe is long, but it bends towards justice.
—Rev. Martin Luther King Jr.

Notwithstanding their pleasures and relations, all men must suffer in due time the fruit of their works; as a coconut detaching itself from its stalk falls down, so life will end when its time is spent.
— Sutra Kritanga

Dada, could you explain the law of karma?

The law of *karma*, simply stated, is the law of cause and effect. It is a scientific law. It is a universal law. It is built up of two universal laws: (1) As you think, so you become; and (2) as you sow, so shall you reap. You cannot sow thorns and reap apples. The law of *karma* is universal in its application. It applies equally to all. We are sowing seeds everyday in the field of life. Every thought I think, every word I utter, every deed I perform, every emotion I arouse within me, every feeling, fancy, wish, that awakens within me, are seeds I am sowing in the field of life. In due course, the seeds will germinate and grow into trees, and yield fruit— bitter or sweet— which I shall have to eat. No one else can do that for me.

There are causes that produce their effect immediately. There are other causes that produce their effect after a long time.

As an example, if you go to a party and overeat, it is a cause you have created. This cause produces an immediate effect— acute indigestion. There are other causes which take very long to produce their effect. But every cause must produce its effect, every seed must yield its fruit. This, in simple words, is the law of *karma*.

Are we not all born equal?

We are told, all men are created equal. No one can be so blind or foolish as to imagine that there is actual equality of ability or environment or conditions of birth for all. Why, in the same family, all children do not have equality of ability or intelligence. There is a family of which the eldest son is an IAS officer and the younger is unable to pass the SSC examination. We have a proverb in Sindhi which says, "The mother gives birth to children, each brings with himself his own destiny." In other words, each one brings his *karma* with himself. There is a family of which the youngest son is a multi millionaire, while the eldest is so poor that he and his children are virtually starving, literally begging for food.

Two questions arise: 1) Is this inequality the result of *karma*? 2) And if so, is it fair? The answer to both, as the great teachers of India have taught us, is in the affirmative. You are the architect of your own destiny. You are the builder of your own fate. Every thought, emotion, wish, action creates *karma*: we have been creating *karma* for thousands, perhaps millions of years. If our thoughts, emotions and actions are benevolent, so-called good *karma* results. If they are malevolent, evil or difficult, bad *karma* is created. The good or evil we generate attaches its effect to us and remains in our life-current until we have satisfied it by balancing it out.

Why are our past karmas kept a secret from us?

Don't you think it is a great mercy of God that our *karmic* links are not known to us? Else, it may be difficult for us to live in the world. Thus, for instance, there may be a man whose wife, in the present incarnation, was his bitter enemy in an earlier incarnation and has now become his wife only to settle previous accounts. If all this were revealed to us, what would be our condition?

How did bad karma originate?

Man was given free will, he was given the right of choice. He can choose between what the *Upanishads* call *preya* and *shreya*. *Preya* is the pleasant: the path of *preya* is the path of pleasure that lures us but leads to our degradation. As a Danish proverb has it, "After pleasant scratching comes unpleasant smarting."

Shreya is the good. The path of *shreya* may, at first, be difficult to tread but ultimately leads to our betterment and well-being and spiritual unfolding. At every step, man is given this choice. Many of us, alas, choose the easy path, the path of pleasure and so keep on multiplying undesirable *karma*.

If all that happens today is the result of our past karmas, does it mean that everything is pre-destined?

No, certainly not! We are the architects of our own destiny, the builders of our own future. Many of us blame fate, *kismet* for our misfortune. But let me tell you, that you are the builders of your own fate. Therefore, be careful, especially, of your thoughts. We pay scant attention to our thoughts, believing that they are of no consequence. We say, after all, it was only a thought, what does it matter? Every thought is a seed you are sowing in the field of life, and what you sow today, you will have to reap in the near or remote future.

God has created a universe of beauty, fullness, happiness and harmony. Each one of us is a child of God. God wishes each one of us to be happy, healthy, prosperous, successful and to enjoy all the good things He has created. We keep ourselves away from all those bounties because of our *karma*. Change your *karma* and you will change the conditions in which you live. And you can change your *karma* by adopting a new pattern of thinking.

Dada, can karmas be wiped off by japa?

It is believed that the effects of *karma* can be mitigated through *Nama japa*. In any case, the suffering can be reduced, because *Nama japa* acts as a sort of chloroform. It is like going through an operation. The surgeon puts you under anesthesia and you come out of the operation without feeling the acute pain. Else the pain is so excruciating, that a person could die of it. This is what *Nama japa* does to you.

Can saints take over the karma of their disciples?

They can. However, normally, they do not wish to interfere with the law of *karma*. For they know that it is not punitive but reformative. The law of *karma* does not wish to punish us for what we may have done in the past. The law of *karma* wishes to reform us and so sends us experiences which may help our spiritual advancement. It is true there have been cases when men of God have taken the *karmas* of their devotees upon themselves. It is like having birds released from their cages. A man may purchase the birds and set them free. Likewise, a man who is rich in the wealth of the spirit may, if he so desires, pay for our *karma* and release us from the cage of *maya*.

Does man get mukti (liberation from the cycle of birth and death) after working out his karma?

Karma leads to karma, the process of sowing and reaping goes on, endlessly. But *mukti*, liberation, comes through the grace of God. Thus we have cases of sinners being suddenly transformed into saints. It was a Christian saint who said, "What God is by nature, man becomes by grace." Through grace, man becomes Godlike, emancipated, free!

How may we live a life that bears witness to the law of karma?

Let me pass on to you a few practical suggestions:

1. Always be aware of your thoughts. As you think, so you become. Every time an evil thought approaches you, push it out of your mind. An effective way of pushing out a thought is to slap or pinch yourself the moment an undesirable thought enters your mind.

2. As you sow, so shall you reap. Therefore, be aware of every little thing that you do. Everyday, spend some time in silence, preferably at the same time and at the same place. Sitting in silence, go over all that you did during the earlier twenty four

hours. It is helpful if you go over your actions in the reverse order, i.e., think first of what you did a little while ago, then of what you did a little while earlier, and so on. You will surely find that there were things which you did which you should not have done as there are things which you did not do but should have done— many errors of commission and omission. Repent for them all and pray to the Lord for wisdom and strength never to do similar things again.

3. Take care of your *sanga*— the people with whom you associate. If you move in the company of holy ones, something of their holiness will penetrate your life and fill you with holy aspirations and vibrations. Hence the value of daily *satsang*.

4. Develop the spirit of detachment. Attend to your duties and be inwardly detached, knowing that nothing, nobody belongs to you. You are only an actor— and also a spectator— in the ever-unfolding, cosmic drama of life. You have to play this double role of an actor and a spectator.

5. Grow in the spirit of surrender to God, "Not my will, but Thy Will be done, O Lord!" Repeat the divine Name, and pray with a sincere heart that you may rise above the *dwandas*— the pairs of opposites— above pleasure and pain, loss and gain, for it is only then that suffering will not be able to touch you— and you shall be at peace with yourself and with those around you.

6. Be vigilant. Be watchful, live in awareness all the time. It was the Buddha who said to his disciples on one occasion, "O *bhikkhus*, if you are not vigilant, desire will enter your heart even as rain enters a room through a leaky roof."

7. Do as much good as you can, to as many as you can, in as many ways as you can. Help as many as you can, to lift the load on

the rough road of life. The day on which we have not helped a brother here, a sister there, a bird here, an animal there, is a lost day, indeed.

Is there no short cut to the ending of karma?

Yes. There are three ways. The first is the way of self-inquiry, to understand who you are. You are not the body, nor the mind. You are not the *buddhi*. You are that which cannot be touched by *karma*. Once you arrive at that stage, all *karma* drops out.

The other is the way of self-surrender.

The third is the way of selfless service.

Those are the three ways by which the store of *karma* can be burnt. But even then, the '*pralabdha karma*' that you have brought has to be worked out. But the *sanchita karma*, the storehouse of *karma* gets burnt.

But Dada, it is very difficult for young people to accept these three points.

Then we have to keep entering in the cycle of birth and death, until it becomes easy for us to do it. Experience teaches us. We have to pass through those experiences. Very few learn through vicarious experiences.

A parent says to the child, "My child, never do this. I did this and I repented." The child will not understand. He would like to do that and, from his own experience learn, what it is to repent after doing a particular thing. But there are some who learn from vicarious experience.

This whole life is a jail. We are prisoners. We think we are free but we are in bondage. We need to be liberated. To get *mukti*, you need *mumukshatva*, the desire, the intense longing, for liberation. That is very necessary. Until that arises, you don't want to be liberated. You are happy and satisfied with whatever life gives you.

There was a man. They asked him, "Why don't you desire to go to heaven?" He said, "Life must be boring there. Here it is exciting."

In the law of evolution, can a human being be re-born as an animal?

When the law of *karma* finds that a person is so incorrigible that he will not be reformed until he goes back to the stage of the animal, and begins again— it is only in such cases that a human being is re-born as an animal.

I sometimes think about a classmate of mine. When I was in the first standard, he was in the fourth. I came to the second, he was still in the fourth standard. I went to the third and he continued to be in the fourth. I went to the fourth and he was my classmate. I went to the fifth and the teachers said, "We must do something. This boy has been in the fourth standard for so many years, let us send him back to the third, so that he can gather some momentum."

I do not feel that anyone of you could have had that experience. But it does happen in very few cases, where people commit mortal crimes, for example, kill little children. Then perhaps, the law of *karma* gives us the body of an animal so that we can restart the process. But it is always for our own good.

If everything that happens to us is ordained by God, then how are we responsible for our actions?

So long as man has the egoistic feeling in his mind that he is the doer, he is responsible for his own actions. When he frees himself from the ego, transcends this feeling of doing, he becomes an instrument of God and all the responsibility for his actions belong to God.

Sadhu Vaswani has said that the principle of karma is that of a boomerang. Could you please explain?

There is an inviolable law which governs the universe from end to end. What you send, comes back to you! Do you gossip about another? You will be gossiped about! Do you send out thoughts of hatred and enmity to another? Hatred and enmity will come back to you, turning your life into a veritable hell! Do you send out loving thoughts to others? Do you pray for struggling souls? Do you serve those that are in need? Are you kind to passers-by, the pilgrims on the way who seek your hospitality? Then remember, sure as the sun rises in the east, all these things will return to you, making your life beautiful and bright as a rose garden in the season of spring!

Dear Dada, how do we know in any situation that it is God's Will taking effect and not our will?

There are certain things that happen to us. We do not want them to happen and try to avoid or escape them. But inspite of all our efforts, things happen. Those are the things that we should accept as God's Will. It is something that I did not want to happen. Yet it has happened. But there are other things that I do. For instance, I get angry at someone, I go and gossip, I spread wrong reports about a friend. That is my will. I am doing it.

Liberation

I listened to the silence of the night and I felt as if I had all of a sudden penetrated the very heart of the universe. An immense happiness, such as I had never known, swept over me with a flow of fulfillment.
– Carlo Levi

But when Thou O Lord shalt command,
Then only shall I be released from self.
– Mechthild of Magdeburg

You know that you know nothing.
Find out that knowledge. That is liberation (Mukti).
– Sri Ramana Maharishi

How can I attain emancipation?

The easiest way is the way of surrender. *Sarvadharman parityaja mamekam sharanam vrija.*" Renouncing all rites and writ duties, come unto Me for single refuge, O Arjuna, and I shall liberate you from all bondage to sin and suffering, of this have no doubt!"

We are told we should be desireless but to wish to be desireless is also a desire, isn't it?

To wish to be desireless is not a desire. It is an aspiration of the heart. There is a difference between desire and aspiration. Aspiration is something that lifts you up. Desire is gravitation, it pulls you down. Aspiration is levitation, it takes you up. Desire binds, whereas aspiration liberates.

How may we escape from the cycle of birth and death?

There are many ways in which we may seek liberation from the cycle of birth and death. One way is to enter within, behold the light, hear the *shabad*, and be one with that light and sound. This will liberate you forever.

There is also the way of selfless service. When you go out to serve those in need, but seek nothing in return, not even a word of thanks, then you are freed from the self and move closer to liberation.

Then there is the way of surrender. You surrender yourself totally to the Will of the Master, the Will of the Lord. You accept all life's experiences as His *prasad* and you don't complain. This is in itself liberation.

Yet another way, is the way of self-enquiry. Enter into the depths within you. Ask yourself again and again, "What am I?" You will soon realise that you are not the body you wear. It is only a garment that you have worn. Nor are you the mind or the intellect. Then what are you? As you probe deeper and deeper, you will touch the plane of the pure white light— the radiance that casts no shadow and you will be free, liberated from the cycle of birth and death.

Sri Krishna says in the Bhagavad Gita that this material world is a prison house and everyone has to experience four things— birth, disease, old age and death. Then how do we attain liberation?

Sri Krishna also says that it is through the human birth that you can attain to freedom. Each one of us has been given this golden opportunity of the human birth which is a gateway to freedom, emancipation, liberation. Sri Krishna also says that there are four gifts of life. Sir Krishna calls them: *artha, kama, dharma, moksha*. It is for you to choose between making this world a prison-house or a gateway to liberation.

There is a beautiful story about a blind man who found himself locked up in a hall which had eighty-four doors. The blind man wanted to come out of the hall. He was informed that eighty-three doors were closed, only one door was open. It was for him to find the open door and come out. He kept on touching the wall as he walked step by step. He came to the first door and found it closed. He moved further to the second door, to the third, and so on. He found that they were closed. Just as he arrived at the open door, there was an itching sensation on the palm of his hand, so he took the hands off the wall and started scratching them and in the process, passed by the open door, missing it completely.

This is our condition. We all are blind people. We have had to pass through countless *junees* (births) and now have been born as human beings. The human body is as an open door. But, alas! each one of us feels some itch or the other. Some feel the itch to gamble, some to pleasure, some to power and in the process, this golden opportunity of the human birth slips through our fingers. It is only through the human birth that one can achieve liberation.

So it is up to you to make this world a prison house or to make it a door which will lead you to liberation, to *moksha*.

Life

Oftentimes the test of courage becomes rather to live than to die.
— *Alfieri*

Everyman's life is a fairytale written by God.
— *Hans Christian Anderson*

Dost thou love life? Then do not squander time,
for that is the stuff life is made of.
— *Franklin*

As is a tale, so is life: not how long it is,
but how good it is, is what matters.
— *Seneca*

What is the purpose of life?

The purpose of man's life is to grow in purity and perfection. Blessed are the pure in heart, for they shall see God! He who has a vision of God in the heart within, beholds God wherever he turns— in every atom of an atom. And he makes the discovery that though God dwells within man, men know it not and so are unhappy. And he says to himself, I shall be a servant of all who suffer and are in pain! The purpose of life is that it may be poured out as a sacrifice on the altar of suffering creation.

Dada, how may we have real fun out of life?

To get real fun out of life, you must:

1. Throw out the fun-killers that you carry about with yourselves all the time. Three of them are lust, greed and hatred.

2. Never think or talk negatively. And do not anticipate troubles which may never come at all. Be positive.

3. Fill your heart with love— love of God, fellow-men, birds and animals, nature and yourself.

4. Keep yourself active all the time. The best and noblest of actions is to bring comfort to the comfortless.

5. See the good in everyone. Be blind to the faults of others.

6. In everything that you do, pour the best that is in you. Therefore, work not for wages, work for love.

7. Be a master over circumstances and over your desires and animal appetites.

8. Let go, let go, let God! Let go of everything. Let God take charge of your life and affairs. Letting go permits divine ideas to flow, divine power to work, divine order to bless your mind, body and affairs.

You say that life is wonderful. How can we change our lives to make it wonderful?

Life can be changed. Life must be changed. Just think of joy, love and peace, purity and prosperity and your environment will shape itself in accordance with your persistent thinking. Let me offer you a few practical tips to make your life truly wonderful.

1. Realise what you are in essence.
2. Count your blessings.
3. Become a thank you person.
4. Keep the gate closed on the past.
5. Make today count.
6. Trust in the goodness and caring power of God.
7. Let go, let go, let God.

Can you offer us some golden rules of life?

One golden rule given since time immemorial is: Do unto others as you would have others do unto you. Another is: Each person must do his or her own duty. Today people claim their rights but I ask you, what about your duties? In the *Bhagavad Gita*, the word for duty is *swadharma*. This word is repeated over and over again in the *Gita*, but nowhere is there a mention of the word, 'right'.

If we all do our duty, then rights will automatically be taken care of. The cosmic drama will be successful only if each of us plays his own role. If I do my duty in the right way, the portals of perfection will be open to me.

Yet another golden rule is: Do your duty and a little more. Humanity is one family. Therefore help as many as you can, as much as you can.

Love

Love is an endless mystery, for it has nothing else to explain it.
– Rabindranath Tagore

The world's greatest need is— Love-in-Action.
– J.P. Vaswani

Why do two people in love suddenly feel they hate each other?

Love is a great giver and does not want anything in return. You get a little pleasure and you think you are in love. After a year, when someone asks you, "How is that person?" You say, "O, I hate him!" Now how can you turn love into hate? Love cannot turn into hate. You loved him because you had that sensation, that pleasurable sensation. You hate him because you no longer get that sensation. Love must not be confounded with sensation or sexual attraction. Love is of God. Love is God. Love is not an attribute of God, but God Himself. But it should be true love, like Majnu's love for Laila. When you develop such love, then it can never turn into hate.

Dada, how may we grow in divine love?

Following are the practical suggestions on how to grow in divine love:

1. You must fall— or rather rise— in love with God. Therefore it is necessary to establish some relationship with God. Make God your father or mother or brother or friend or master or the heart's beloved. Let everything you do strengthen this relationship with God.

2. Live with God all the time. Therefore talk to him, again and again. Engage yourself in a loving, humble, intimate conversation with God.

3. Speak softly. Treat everyone with love and kindness. Do not see the faults of others. For every blow you receive, give back a blessing.

4. He who loves God, fears to do anything which may displease God. He strives to live a life of purity.

5. Whatever you do, do it for the pure love of God.

6. The law of love is the law of service and sacrifice. Go out of your way to help others. And rejoice in the Will of God.

Can love affect the physical body?

Today psychologists have proved that the effects of love and peace of mind on the physical body can be measured. An unloved infant will have retarded bone growth and may even die. An infant that receives love grows faster. Love and peace of mind keep us healthy and help us in facing the problems of daily life in the right spirit. They provide the courage we need to confront each day and utilise unpleasant experiences as motivators.

How do you explain unrequited love?

Unrequited love can be explained in terms of the law of *karma*. All give and take is balanced. This life is only a micropart of the entire film. What you see is a part, not the whole. It is a great law of the universe that what you give out, comes back to you ultimately. Nothing is lost. You might have already received what you are giving now.

There is another aspect to it. Disillusionment with human relationships is a part of life-experience, necessary for evolution.

You have said, "Love is not blind. Lovers are blind." What does this mean? And, why is it good to be blind?

When you become a lover, you forget everything. You are prepared to sacrifice everything for the beloved. If you are a lover of truth and beauty, goodness and perfection, then it is good to be blind.

Dadaji, you say that love is God. Then why is there jealousy and selfishness in love nowadays?

Wherever there is jealousy, or selfishness, there is lack of love. Real love is not there. Like I said, love is a liberator. Love does not wish to imprison the person it loves. What we popularly call love is not love in the true sense of the term.

The test of love is sacrifice. How much are you able to sacrifice for the sake of him whom you love or for the sake of her whom you love? If you are prepared to sacrifice your all, that is true love. If not, it is not love. It is passion.

Passion is jealous, and selfish and possessive. True love comes to liberate, to set us free. True love does not demand anything. In fact, it is prepared to give everything.

There is a beautiful incident in the life of Majnu and Laila. We are told that one day, a camel driver happened to pass through Majnu's village. On enquiry, Majnu learnt that the destination of the camel driver was the town in which Laila lived. So he said to the camel driver, "If I give you a message for Laila, will you take it to her?" The camel driver said willingly, "I will do it."

Majnu started giving the message. The message went on and on. It was endless! The camel driver said, "I have to get back in time. Your message seems to be unending! So I will get on the camel. I will ride on, you follow behind me giving me your message. As soon as the message is over, you may return and I will go to Laila's town and deliver the entire message."

Majnu followed the camel but the message would not end. It went on, until they arrived at Laila's town. They learnt that on that day Laila was entertaining some beggars and would be giving alms. Majnu, too, joined the line of beggars with a cup in his hand. When it was Majnu's turn, Laila took the cup and smashed it to the ground. The cup broke into pieces.

Majnu began to dance in a rapture of ecstasy. The people said to him, "You had only one cup, and that also Laila has broken into pieces. To the other beggars she gave something or the other. And you are dancing in joy, what is the reason ?" He said, "The reason is a very simple one. Laila meant to teach the one supreme lesson that to enter into the life of true love the body must be transcended. The cup symbolised the human body and she broke it into pieces. It is only when we transcend the human body that we will know what true love is.

One body touches another, we get a sensation and we think that love is beautiful. That is not love. That is imprisonment. You only get imprisoned. One of the two, whose bodies come together, gets tired of the other body. That one runs after a third body. Do you call that love? Therefore true love is that which transcends the human body. And that love is divine. That love is universal. It moves out to all.

Dadaji, what exactly is wrong with me if I find myself falling in love, and falling out of love every now and then? How do I know what is the final time I fall in love?

Since you are a student, it is your *swadharma*, your duty, to study, not to fall in and out of love. If a student ventures into the field of love, he will fall in and out of it. The student must study. The right time comes when a man thinks of falling in or out of love, not before that.

A little boy, eight years old, told me that he was in love with a girl. I asked him, "Who is that girl?" I thought it was his teacher because when we were small we used to fall in love with our teachers. He said, "She studies in the school, just one class lower than me." I was shocked. I asked, "How do you express your love?" He said, "I call her on the phone and we keep on talking to each other for an hour or two at a time." Be true to your *swadharma*, do not chase love. Rather let true love find you.

Marriage

In marriage, being the right person is as important as finding the right person.
– Wilburt Donald Gouch

A happy marriage is the union of two good forgivers.
– Robert Quillen

Is marriage a necessary institution?

Marriage is not just an institution, it is a sacrament, a sacred union. It was after centuries of experience that the wise ones of ancient times formulated the rules of marriage. Nowadays we have chaos in society. There is no respect for the sanctity of marriage.

Just as there are traffic laws, which have to be followed to avoid accidents, similarly there are laws of marriage. When you get married, your life is regulated by certain rules. Freedom is not doing what you like. Freedom is the ability to do what you should do.

When the choice is between our own happiness and our parents' happiness, what should we choose?

Your happiness depends on your parents, but you will realise this much later. At the moment you may think that parents are fools. But later on, you will realise that the advice they gave you was perfect.

Is there any one factor which can make a marriage last?

For a marriage to last there must be harmony which does not depend on external things. More important than physical beauty is the nature of a person. And it is only when you live together, rub shoulders with each other, that your true nature is revealed.

A girl came to me and said, "I want to marry a particular person."

"Can you describe the person to me?" I asked her.

"He belongs to an aristocratic family," she said,

"That is zero," I said to her.

"He holds a doctorate in computer science."

"Another zero," I said to her.

"He is the only son, the only child of his parents."

"Yet another zero," I said to her.

"He is so handsome," she continued.

"One more zero," I said.

The zeros went on multiplying. Until finally, she said, "He is a man with sterling qualities of character and faith in God."

"If that is so," I said to her, "then put one in front of all the zeros and he will score that many marks."

You must study the temperament of the individual and see how far your temperaments will be in harmony with each other.

This is what will make a marriage last.

How do you judge the character of your partner in an arranged marriage?

It is very difficult to judge the character of an individual. Therefore, it is the duty of your parents to make adequate enquiries and verify the facts.

Should I tell my future husband that I had loved someone else earlier?

If you like you can tell your future husband, but it is not necessary at all. It might unnecessarily upset him, disturb him. May be you have loved someone before, but your fiancee may have loved many girls before.

When couples come to me for advice, I tell them forget the past but from now on let your life be an open book to your life partner.

What makes a marriage successful?

The word for the married state in our ancient Sanskrit language is *grahasta ashrama*. Marriage is an *ashrama*— a place of discipline,

Marriage is not a licence. It is at once a discipline and a responsibility. In marriage two persons— a man and a woman— offer the whole of their mind, body, and feelings to each other. They do not live for self alone: they live for each other. Success in marriage is more than finding the right person. Being the right person is even more important.

What is the purpose served by marriage?

Men and women were created by God so that they could form one complete whole. So it is that God endowed men with certain qualities and women with complementary qualities. By themselves, neither man nor woman are complete. Men have strength, determination, energy, vigour, guts. Women have great sensibility, spiritual aspirations, the spirit of sympathy, service and sacrifice. Men rely on their intellect. Women have intuition. Rudyard Kipling said, "A woman's guess is much more accurate than a man's certainty." Man and woman together form one complete person. By themselves, both are incomplete. Each needs the other. Each has to learn much from the other.

A holy man said, "Except a man become a woman, he cannot enter the Kingdom of heaven. And except a woman become a man, she cannot enter the Kingdom of heaven." Love may begin with physical attraction but marriage, in due course, fuses them together so that they form one complete whole. This is the purpose of marriage. When we forget it, we lose the proper perspective of marriage. I am afraid, today there are too many couples who may be classified as married strangers. They may share the same house, the same table, the same car and yet may actually be drifting away from each other.

Dada, if marriages are made in heaven, divorces must be made in heaven too?

No! No! No! No! No!

I think divorce is against the law of God. Divorce is very much like suicide. Marriages are made in heaven. They cannot be broken on earth. But if man uses his discretion and breaks a marriage, he has to pay for it in due course.

If a couple can't get along and are a burden to each other, why not opt for divorce?

The very first important word in the theory of *Karma* as explained by Sri Krishna in the *Bhagavad Gita* is *swadharma*. To thy own *dharma*, you must be true. To your duty, you must be true. Very often, there is a conflict between duty and personal desire. But I have to be true to my duty.

Stretching your example a little further, suppose your mother (who has brought you up) has fallen sick. She has become a burden on you. Will you give her up? Why? Because it is your duty to take care of your mother. Likewise, if marriage is a sacrament (it is regarded as a *sanskara*) it cannot be broken. The wife may prove to be a burden on the husband. The husband may prove to be a burden on the wife, but it cannot be broken. They have to work out their *karma*. Man has been given utmost freedom. God has given man the same freedom which he has kept for Himself. But God does not interfere with the law of *karma*. So for everything that man does, he is responsible. He is sowing a seed. That seed will germinate, grow into a tree and bear fruit. Whatever be the fruit— bitter, sweet, sour— it has to be eaten by man.

For a woman, who should come first— the Lord or her husband?

That depends on the woman! If she is like Mirabai, she places the Lord above the husband, and she does not hide this fact from the husband! But every woman must see that she does nothing to incur

ation *Violent*
Egoism. *Violent* *Silence* *Spi*
Seeker *Service* *Silence* *Spi*
brations *Willpower* *Woman* *Of The World* *Bhagavad* 9.
Selfishness, *Frustration,*
Rituals *Sadhu* *Vaswant*
Thought-Power *Understand*
Education *Faith* *Fear* *For*
Meditation M
And

the displeasure of her husband. Let me add, every husband must see to it that he does not incur the displeasure of his wife.

If a man and a woman get married and then they decide to divorce each other, is the woman entitled to a chance of getting married again?

I don't believe in divorce. I believe marriage is a sacrament. It is something sacred. It must not be broken because, I believe, in the law of *karma*. So the question of a second marriage does not arise.

What about couples who are incompatible?

The greatest famine in the world is the famine of understanding. No two people seem to understand each other.

Today, people speak of emotional incompatibility. It is a myth invented by jurists and lawyers so that they may be able to argue in favour of divorce.

There are no emotional incompatibilities. There are only misunderstandings and mistakes which can be corrected where there is the will to do so.

How may we avoid being married strangers? How may we, after marriage, be fused into one complete whole?

Let me pass on to you ten practical suggestions. I sometimes refer to them as the ten commandments of marriage.

1. The very first commandment is, avoid the next quarrel. If one of you is in a mood to quarrel, the other one should be patient. His or her turn will come at the right time. But both should not lose their temper at the same time.

2. The second commandment of marriage is, be a good listener. Listen to what the other person has to say. We like to talk but are

not prepared to listen. Let us be good listeners. Of a couple it was said, in the days of courtship he talked and she listened. On their honeymoon, she talked and he listened. Now that they are settled down in their own home, both talk and the neighbours listen."

3. The third commandment of marriage is, appreciate your spouse. Everyone loves to be appreciated. Do not find fault with your spouse when you are in the midst of other people. Leonardo da Vinci said, "Reprove your friend in secret, praise him before others." When we appreciate others, we help to draw out the best in them.

4. The fourth commandment is, keep your love fresh! After marriage, spouses take each other for granted. Women have complained to me, "There was a time when our husbands gave us many promises, made many vows, took great interest in what we did. All this has become a part of history. Now they take us for granted." Therefore, keep your love fresh.

5. The fifth commandment is, do not expect perfection of each other. No man or woman is ever perfect. It was Jesus who said, "Call me not perfect. Alone the Father in heaven is perfect!" Marriage involves two imperfect human beings joining together. Accept your spouse for what he or she is, not for what he or she would be, could be or should be.

6. The sixth commandment is, be a good forgiver. To make marriage a success, to make it a source of happiness and harmony, you have to forgive much. It is the prerogative of marriage to give and give and give— and forgive— and never be tired of giving and forgiving. "How many times shall I forgive?" asked a husband. "Shall I forgive seven times?" "No", came the answer, "you must forgive seventy times seven." 70 times 7 is

490 times which means you must forgive without counting. And a wife complained, "I have been forgiving until I can forgive no longer. I have forgiven and received nothing in return." And she was told, "Continue to forgive without expecting anything in return."

7. The seventh commandment of marriage is, you must be patient, loving, understanding, kind and true to each other.

8. The eighth commandment is, develop a healthy sense of humour. If two people have to live with each other, they must develop a healthy sense of humour. They must learn to laugh and make each other laugh.

9. The ninth commandment is, if ever there is a misunderstanding, do not hide your feelings. Do not hesitate in discussing whatever is in your hearts, freely and without fear.

10. The tenth and the most important commandment is, everyday, you must find time to sit together and praise the Lord and thank Him for having brought the two of you together.

Meditation

Silence is the garden of meditation.
– 'Ali

Nowhere can man find a quieter or more untroubled retreat than in his own soul.
– Marcus Aurelius

Cultivating solitude, eating lightly, restraining speech, body and mind, constantly devoted to the discipline of meditation.
– Bhagavad Gita

Meditate every day. And you will pass, gradually, into a new consciousness of at-one-ment with all. For in all is the One Life. There is nothing dead. Pure matter is pure abstraction.
– Sadhu Vaswani

Dadaji, how does a beginner learn to meditate?

To meditate you must first learn to concentrate.

Concentrate on one idea, one thought, one object, one Name. When you have grown in concentration, then meditation becomes very easy. I sit in the lotus posture; I close my eyes and try to meditate. But because I have not yet learnt concentration, my mind wavers. It keeps on drifting from one thought to another. So concentration is the first step on the path of meditation.

How can we grow in concentration?

The question has been answered in the *Bhagavad Gita*. Arjuna puts this question to the Master. "The mind is more restless than a storm. Will I be able to control it?" And Sri Krishna says, "It may not be easy to control the mind but it is possible. You can control the mind by these two means, *abhyasa* and *vairagya*."

Abhyasa is doing the same thing over and over again. We are slaves to our habits which have become a part of our nature. Now we have to form or reform new habits.

Vairagya is the spirit of detachment. You realise that all that you see, all that you touch, all that you conceive is passing, it has no value.

Dada, can you suggest some practical exercises for concentration?

There is one very simple exercise in concentration. Let the candle flame be burning in front of you. Keep it at eye level and keep on looking at the candle flame. After a while, close your eyes and try to concentrate on the flame. You will see the candle flame burning in your mind's eye. Then gradually it will fade away. Again open your eyes and repeat the exercise. You could also do a similar exercise with a picture of your *Ishtadeva*— Sri Krishna, Mahadeva or Sri Rama, Jesus, Guru Nanak, Baha'u'llah, Buddha. Keep a picture at eye level, open your eyes, and concentrate on the form. Then, close your eyes. You will see that form for a little while, and then it will fade away. Keep on doing it. You will grow in concentration.

There is yet another exercise which is known as *tratak*. It is keeping your eyes fixed on a candle flame, but you must not blink. The eyes must be open all the time. Water will flow out of your eyes. It is as though you are weeping, shedding tears, but you should not close your eyes. As you do this, you will grow in concentration.

Concentration is the very foundation of meditation.

Can listening to instrumental music help in meditation?

It can. There is a type of meditation based on music. There are a number of *Sufi* saints who tell us that music can take you to the seventh plane. But it should be music of the right type, music which should wake up the dormant spirit within you.

Dada, sometimes we reach or achieve higher levels for short periods of time but fall down again. What should we do to sustain further?

I think what is needed is inner purification. If only you can purify yourself, all these experiences that make you feel that you have reached certain spiritual heights, all these experiences will become natural. You shouldn't strive to achieve certain experiences. All you need to strive for is inner purification. Purity is going to take you to that point. Blessed are the pure in heart for they shall see God. But the spiritual path is very much like a mountain climb. When you climb a mountain, you go up but again you have to pass through a valley to be able to rise still higher. So when you are in the valley, be not depressed. It is only a part of the path that will lead you to the highest.

If I sleep less, and I sit in meditation, I feel drowsy and even go to

sleep and dream.

You must not sleep less but you must sleep well. Whatever work you do, you should do it well. When you meditate, you should meditate. When you sleep, you should sleep. When you get up from your sleep and find that you are drowsy, it only means that you need more sleep. You should not meditate when you are feeling drowsy, because then you will not be able to meditate, you will vegetate. When you sit to meditate, you must have a feeling of freshness.

Dada, can you offer us some guidelines for meditation?

Meditation is being regarded now, by an ever increasing number of scientists, as a 20th and 21st century medicine. Their research has shown that meditation alters the activity of the nervous system in such a way that the creative energy of the individual is recharged.

Success in meditation is closely related to peaceful living. For meditation to be fruitful, the mind must be calm, and for that it is necessary for man to conduct his normal life and activities in a peaceful, loving manner.

Following are the practical suggestions on how to meditate:

1. Sit in silence in an easy and comfortable posture with the spinal cord, the neck and head in a straight line.

2. Practise meditation preferably at the same place and at the same time, everyday.

3. Sit facing the east or the north.

4. Go to God as you are— with your sins and imperfections.

5. Think of an object or a symbol or an incident from the life of a great one.

6. As you sit in silence, wear a soft smile.

7.   Let your daily life be one of sacrifice.

Dada, is not meditation meant for those who have nothing to do with the work-a-day world?

The life of meditation is not the life of a hermit, which keeps us aloof from our fellow-men. Rather, through meditation, our sympathies are quickened, our perceptions grow keener, our feelings deepen, we grow in unselfishness and perform our duties with greater efficiency. Through meditation we contact a source of tremendous power which is within each one of us but of which many of us are not aware.

I believe that a few minutes of meditation everyday is essential for peace of mind. However, I have a tough time clearing my mind of all thoughts and simply cannot focus on the Supreme Lord. How can I tackle this problem?

The mind has acquired this habit of wandering— not through this birth merely, but through birth after birth. Let me tell you the story of *Mullah* Nasruddin. He would sit everyday for eight hours, in silence, with his ear against the wall. He did this day after day.

One day, his wife asked him, "*Mullah*, you sit with your ear stuck to the wall everyday. Tell me, what do you hear?

The *Mullah* replied, "If you wish to hear what I hear, you must come and sit here yourself." Next morning, the wife got up very early and prepared the day's meals quickly, so that she would be free to go and sit all day with her ear against the wall. She sat for four long hours— but she heard nothing.

Exasperated, she said to the *Mullah*, "I have sat here for four hours and I have heard nothing. I am tired and I am giving up now."

The *Mullah* retorted, "You want to give up after four hours. I have

tion Life Violent Dreams Worry. Science
geism, Silence Spirituality Woman Yoga
eeker Service Silence Willpower Woman Bhagavad Gita Faith Ferg
Of The World Selfishness, Frustration, Sadhu Vaswani Understanding
Rituals Thought Power Education Faith Fear Forg
And G Meditation Mi

been sitting thus for 8 hours everyday for the last 28 years, I have not heard anything either. But I do not give up!" It is this persistence that you need when you sit in silence!

There is a simple breathing exercise suggested by the Vietnamese Buddhist Master, Thich Nhat Hanh, which may help you to grow in concentration.

1. Close your eyes. Become aware of the breathing process—the going in and coming out of your breath.

2. As you breathe in, say to yourself, "I am aware that the breath is going in." As you breathe out, say to yourself, "I am aware that the breath is coming out." Repeat this five times saying "in" and "out".

3. As you inhale, say to yourself, "I am aware that the breath is becoming deep." As you exhale, say to yourself, "I am aware that my breath is becoming slow." Do this five times repeating, "D-e-e-p", as you inhale, "s-l-o-w" as you exhale.

4. At the next step, say to yourself as you inhale, "I am aware of the present moment as I breathe in." When you exhale, say to yourself, "I know that this moment is perfect." Do this five times repeating "P-r-e-s-e-n-t" as you breathe in; "p-e-r-f-e-c-t", as you breathe out.

5. Repeat the word "c-a-l-m" as you inhale; repeat the word "r-e-l-a-x" as you exhale, five times.

This exercise in breathing will help you considerably with your meditation.

Breathing is with you 24 hours a day— you are never without it, it is your best friend. Use it to harness the power of concentration.

Dada, can you tell us about the type of meditation preached and practised by the Buddha?

The Buddha speaks of five types of meditation. The first is, the meditation of love in which we so adjust our heart that we wish for the happiness of all living things, including the happiness of our enemies.

The Second is, the meditiation of compassion, in which we think of all beings in distress, vividly representing in our imagination their sorrows and anxieties so as to arouse a deep compassion for them within us.

The third is, the meditation of joy in which we think of the prosperity of others and rejoice with their rejoicings.

The fourth is, the meditation on impurity, in which we think of the evil consequences of immorality and corruption. In this meditation, we realise how trivial is the pleasure of the moment and how fatal are its consequences!

The fifth is, the meditation on serenity, in which we rise above love and hate, tyranny and wealth and want, and regard our own fate with impartial calm and perfect tranquility.

Mind

The mind is its own place and in it self
Can make a Heaven of Hell, a Hell of Heaven.
– John Milton

What is the most valuable asset God has given us?

More precious than gold and silver, greater than the greatest wealth, greater than any asset, is the mind. In your mind, you have a 24-hour friend. You may be alone, helpless or in distress, but your mind is ever ready to help you and to guide you to overcome any situation. It is your precious friend, an invaluable asset. Only use it in the right way. Do not let the mind be your master. Let it be a fellow-servant in the service of God and suffering humanity.

How do we train our minds?

Thoughts have power. So let us be careful of our thoughts and utilise all the power available to us in the service of suffering humanity. The brain has been called a "fabulous mechanism". It is about the size of half a grape-fruit but is truly a most wonderful thing. It is capable of recording eight hundred memories per second for seventy five years without exhausting itself. It is a storehouse of between ten billion and one hundred billion pieces of information. Even the most powerful computers in the world have memories that hold only a few million items of accessible information. The human brain retains everything that it takes in and never forgets anything. Even though we don't recall all the information received, everything is on a permanent file in our brain.

If a computer were to be built to match the brain's potential, it would occupy space comparable to the size of one of the tallest buildings in the world— the Empire State Building— and need one billion watts of electrical power to run. The cost would work out to an astronomical figure.

The mind is one of God's most amazing gifts to man. Scientists tell us that we use only one-fiftieth of the brain power available to us. Let us train our minds and ourselves to use this fabulous power in the right way. Therefore, let us take care of our thoughts.

Dada, what exactly is intuition or sixth sense as we call it?

Intuition is the gift of knowing things, understanding things which the mind does not know or understand. Our knowledge is based on what the senses tell us and on what the mind decides. But that may not be the whole truth. The senses very often betray us. The mind often jumps to wrong conclusions. Then it is that intuition takes over. Intuition knows, intuition understands. It is here that women excel men. Men have tuition but they don't have intuition. They have sight but they don't have insight.

Dadaji, you have spoken of shampooing our mind everyday. I would like to ask you to give us a few practical ways of doing this.

Shampooing means cleansing. Now, we need to cleanse our minds, we need to unclutter our minds. Our minds are full of wrong thinking, wrong ideas. The minds of so many of us are negative. We must cleanse them of their negativity. To do this, we must get right down into our consciousness and cleanse ourselves of all those rotten thoughts that hold us captive today— thoughts of impurity, selfishness, greed, lust and hatred.

There are so many who nurture in their minds, thoughts of hatred against others. I remember when I was a school boy, there was a classmate of mine, who started hating me, I don't know why. One night, as I was moving in the street, he took a big stick and aimed it at me. If it had hit me, my legs would have been broken. I was only 11 to 12 years old then. But I did not hate him in return. I went and embraced him and said to him, "What is your difficulty? Have I hurt you? Have I done any harm to you?" Then he said, "I find that you are allowed to enter the house of the girl whom I love and they don't allow me to enter." I told him, "That is not my fault. If you wish, from today I will not go there, I am not interested in her." Then he understood me and hatred turned into friendship.

Our minds should be clean and uncluttered. It is only then that we can hope to be happy. Otherwise, with all those dirty thoughts in the mind within, how can we be at peace with ourselves? Whenever I used to get unwanted thoughts, even though I was sitting in a classroom and the teacher was lecturing, I would immediately slap myself. My classmates sitting near me used to ask me what the matter was. I would say it was a mosquito. But it was an internal mosquito, not an outside one. Therefore, whenever you find a negative or an undesirable thought waking up in the mind within you, slap yourself immediately.

Sadhu Vaswani, as a young boy, used to keep a pin with himself. Whenever he found an undesirable thought waking up within him, he would just pierce the pin into his flesh until the body felt so much pain that the mind would cry out, "Forgive me, forgive me! I will not think such a thought again."

What is the difference between soul and mind?

The mind is an instrument of cognition, of knowing things, knowing the material world. The soul is a ray of God, that which you essentially are. The mind is an instrument with which we know. We try to understand things. The soul is immortal, the mind is mortal. The mind is discursive, the soul is synergic. The soul integrates everything but the mind analyses.

We need the help of the mind in doing our work on the physical plane. That is why we have brought with ourselves the instrument of the mind. Out of God emanate many rays, every ray is a soul. This is what makes all of us one. The soul is universal. The mind is individual, the mind individualises but the soul unites.

How can we quieten the mind?

The easiest way is to engage in a loving and intimate conversation with God. There is another way in which you go over all the things that you have done in the past 24 hours, in the reverse order until you get to the first hour. You will see that there are many things that you should not have done, but which you did, as there are many things you should have done, but which you did not do. They are known as the acts of omission and commission. Ask for God's forgiveness and for the strength and wisdom not to repeat such acts in future.

How may we cultivate the subconscious mind ?

1. Always entertain positive thoughts. Never harbour thoughts of jealousy, hatred or lust.

2. Do not react emotionally to things that happen.

3. Never make any negative suggestions in regard to what you want to be. Thus, for instance, never say, I have a bad memory. This will only lead to loss of memory. Rather say my memory is improving.

4. Never hate or resent people. Let love and forgiveness be the law of your life. Many types of illnesses are caused by intense hatred and resentment.

5. Read books that inspire and uplift you rather than books that feature violence, sex, crime and other acts of viciousness. This is specially important in the case of children and youth.

Is inward beauty a matter of the mind?

Inward beauty, I believe, is beauty of thought, aspirations, prayers. If our thoughts are pure, if our aspirations are pure and beautiful, and desires likewise pure and beautiful, we are beautiful within.

Each one of us gets impure thoughts again and again. Dirty emotions wake up within us. We are sitting at a holy place. Suddenly seemingly out of nowhere, an evil desire wakes up within us. An evil thought comes to us. If we let that thought or emotion stay with us, it will be like a stain on our interior life. It is a blot.

Socrates used to pray again and again, "God, make me beautiful within!" If you desire, if you are eager, if you wish to grow beautiful within, then you must build your life in purity. This is very essential. Every impure impulse, impure thought, impure emotion that wakes up within us, spoils our interior beauty. Therefore, the second step is prayer. Keep on praying again and again if you want to grow beautiful within.

All these years, we have been wandering with the mind, doing nothing, gathering nothing. Instead of letting the mind wander after useless things, pick up a great thought— of a great one. It may be a *sloka* from the *Bhagavad Gita* or a line from the *Sant Bani* or the *Gurbani*. Let us keep on repeating the great thought and try to enter into the depths of the meanings of the words we repeat. This will help considerably in controlling the wandering of the mind.

Negative Emotions

Control your emotion or it will control you.
— Samurai Maxim

The worst man is the one who sees himself as the best.
— 'Ali (c. 600-661)

I. Complexes

Dada, wherein lies true security?

There is no sure security in physical or material things. We live in an insecure world. Our very life hangs by a slender thread. True security belongs to him who has developed a childlike trust in God, the Source of all that a man needs— prosperity, power, peace, strength, wisdom, health, happiness, harmony. He is not from us afar. He does not dwell in a distant star. He is wherever we are. He is here, He is now! All we have to do is to turn to Him, and we shall lack nothing.

Please help me as I feel insecure and inferior when I am around people who are fair, tall and intelligent.

If only you realised that the true value of life does not consist in being tall, fair and intelligent, you will be able to give up this feeling.

Sri Krishna is highly regarded by millions of people all over India, and now, even in western countries, as the greatest man who ever lived on earth. Now this greatest man was shorter than I am. He was only three cubits and a half in height. He was not fair.

So, the true value of life does not consist in these outer things. It is what you are within that matters.

Mahatma Gandhi was not fair. It is your inner self that matters. You must get into contact with your real self, your true self. The *Bhagavad Gita* calls it the Self-Supreme. Within each one of us, remember, there are two selves, the lower self and the higher self.

The lower self is the self of passion and pride, lust and hatred and greed and resentment and ill-will, jealousy and envy. All those baser passions, they go to build up the lower self. Our difficulty is that we have identified ourselves with this lower self which is called the ego-self. It sits on the threshold of our consciousness. It easily catches us, captures us, misleads us, leads us astray. And we grope in the darkness which is our own shadow. This is the tragedy of modern man. He has identified himself with the lower self.

This lower self is very tiny. When you sit in meditation and enter into the depths that are within you, you will realise that this ego, this lower self is a speck of a speck of a speck of a speck of a speck. It is so tiny. Yet in our daily life, we magnify it out of all proportion. We think of it as our own true self. We go to it again and again. We follow its dictates and become its obedient servants. Therefore in this world today, wars and violence, hatred and strife are the result of these baser emotions.

But there is within every one of us, the higher self. A man may be the poorest of the poor, the most wretched, the most miserable of men on earth, yet, he carries within himself that higher self. That is what you are in reality. Truly, this was the purpose of education in ancient India. Not merely to teach students physics, chemistry, biology, mathematics, literature, languages, psychology, economics, history, physiology, and philosophy. The real purpose of education was to reveal to the student what he truly was. This is true knowledge.

Can you tell us something more about the higher self?

True knowledge is to know what you are. You are that higher self which the *Gita* refers to as the *Atman*. You are, each one of you, that higher self. We should keep reminding ourselves, "I am not this, the lower self, I am that, the higher self." This is a very good discipline which each one of us will do well to practise.

Suppose I were to ask you, "Who are you?" You will point to your body. You are not the body. The body is as much as a shawl I have worn. If I tell you J. P. Vaswani is this shawl, you will all laugh at me. But that is what you all are doing everyday.

Identify yourself with that higher self. Keep on reminding yourself, "I am not this, I am That." I have not yet known what That is. But surely I am going to reach It because That is what I am. I am That.

How may we rise above this lower self?

There is a touching story in the life of Gautama Buddha.

Once a man came to him and abused him. He referred to all the bad words in the dictionary. Gautama was silent until the man ran out of bad words. Remember, silence is always stronger than speech. After this man had spoken whatever he wanted to speak, Gautama Buddha quietly asked him, "My brother, tell me, if a person brings a gift to someone but that someone does not accept that gift, to whom will the gift belong?" The man replied, "Of course, it will belong to the man who has brought it." Gautama Buddha replied, "All these words that you have brought to me, I do not accept."

Identify yourself with the higher self. How long will you remain a slave to the lower self? You have heard the name of Enrico Caruso, the great Italian singer. Concerning him, Thomas Burke, the great music critic said, "Caruso was not a mere singer, he was a miracle." When Caruso began his career, he was a failure. When he gave his first performance, the Italian people were so badly disappointed that they actually took up sticks in their hands and chased him out of the city. The Italians can be very rough if they want to. But Caruso was not the one to give up. He was found pacing up and down in his room uttering words which became to him the *mantra* of his life. What were those words? "You little me, get out of me, you big me, get into me." He kept on uttering those words again and again, until the "little me" left him and the "big me" took over.

If Caruso could become a miracle, so can you. All you have to do is to identify yourself with the 'big me,' with that 'great me,' with that true me, with the Self Supreme that you really are. This is the purpose of meditation. This is the purpose of religion. Religion does not just mean doing an *aarati*. It means putting you in touch with the Higher Self, that you truly are. *Tat twam asi.* Those are the great words of the ancient *rishis*, *Tat twam asi*. That art thou.

You are not a worm crawling on the earth. You are That. Once you realise this truth, gone is the anger, the ill-will, the dissatisfaction with all that is around you.

How can I overcome my physical weaknesses and infirmities?

By keeping your mind fixed on your true self, your higher self. Another thing which helps is the repetition of the Name divine. If you believe in the efficacy of the Name divine, and if you can utter the Name of God as though you are uttering the Name of your own beloved, you will be abundantly blessed. Then you will get so absorbed, so lost in the Name of the Lord, that your nervousness will go.

Yet another way to overcome physical weakness is by divine grace. Therefore, continue to pray to God to pour His grace on you— however unworthy you may be.

God has blessed me with a good career, a loving family and sufficient material comfort. Why is it that I still feel so unfulfilled?

St. Augustine has said, "Our hearts are restless until they seek rest in Thee, O Lord!" Until you reach God, nothing will give rest to your heart— not status, nor money, nor position, nor power, not even your family. This is what some mystics have called "divine discontent". The seed of this discontent is there within the hearts of all— else we would never aspire to God. We long for Him because all the wealth and comforts of the world cannot give us true satisfaction. We will attain it only when we touch the Lotus Feet of the Lord.

Why is it that the person whom I always like, tries to avoid and neglect me?

There were two salesmen who were friends. One of them was in the habit of saying, "Whenever I go to see a customer, I am sure to miss him." And that is what happened. Every time he went to meet a person, he was told that the person had just left the place only two minutes ago.

His friend on the other hand, was in the habit of saying, "Whenever I go to meet a customer, I am sure to find him." And that is what happened in his case. Whenever he went to meet a particular person, he was told that he had reached just in the nick of time and that if he had arrived a couple of minutes later, he would have missed him. So it is all in the mind. You need to change your way of thinking, your way of speaking. Before you can change your way of speaking, you must change your way of thinking because words are thoughts expressed. Our words carry the power of thoughts. If you start saying, I am sure to be loved by the person whom I love, you will release vibrations which will draw him closer to you.

If we are imperfect, it is because God has willed it so. Then, why should we fight our desires? Why should we try to become perfect?

Supposing a lazy man comes to you, begging for alms, you will tell him, "Don't be lazy. You are able-bodied. Go and work for a living." If he were to tell you, "It is my nature to be lazy and poor. Why are you asking me to change my nature?" This attitude is not likely to satisfy you.

We are all here to put forth our best efforts. The ideal before each one of us is the ideal of perfection. It was Jesus who said, "Be ye perfect, even as your Father in heaven is perfect." In order to attain to this ideal of perfection, we have to curb our lower desires and walk the way of self-control. The alternative is to live a lazy life like the beggar I mentioned earlier—to become lazy and refuse to improve our own condition.

II. Selfishness

Are we humans selfish? Why do we remember God only in times of difficulty?

I should say 99.9 percent of people are selfish. There are very few who are truly unselfish. The degree of selfishness may be different, but we are selfish. We always think of our own good. We always think of what we are going to get out of it. How will it react on us? We think of God, only when we are surrounded by difficulties. Difficulties are, in fact, meant to draw us closer to God. There is no difficulty to the man who is close to God. Difficulties are created on account of the distance that is between us and God. But the man who is close to God never feels that he is passing through any difficulty.

There was a *rabbi*. He was delivering a lecture on the teaching of the Torah to a class of Jewish students. They came upon a line which said, "the truly evolved person is even he, who in the midst of the greatest of difficulties, continues to smile." So the students asked the teacher, "If we are surrounded by the greatest of difficulties, how is it possible to smile under those conditions?"

The *rabbi* said to them, "I myself cannot answer this question because I, too cannot smile when I am in the midst of difficulties. I seem to forget how to smile! How can I give you the answer? But there is one man living here in this town, who has faced all types of difficulties. When he was born, he became an orphan within a week's time. Then he broke his leg and so his difficulties continued. He has gone through all sorts of trials, yet he continues to smile. You must go and ask him."

The students went in a row and knocked at the door of this man. When the door was opened, the man asked them the purpose of their visit. The students explained it to him. He said to them, "You have come to a wrong address, because I am one who has had to face no difficulty whatsoever! I am seventy-three years old but in all these seventy-three years, I have not had to face a single difficulty. How can I tell you how to smile in the midst of difficulties?" A true example of a man who lived in proximity with God! Such a person does not regard anything as difficult. So when you think that you are surrounded by troubles, that a difficult experience has come to you, remember, it has come only because you have not yet drawn close enough to God.

What remedy do you suggest to overcome selfishness?

There is only one permanent cure to selfishness and that is self-realisation. When self-realisation comes in, selfishness goes out. There was a boy who was in love with a girl. Her name was May. Everytime he came to meet her, he was told that she had just gone out. Then one day, May's little brother said to this young man, "In our house we will call you June, because when you come May has just left."

It is like that. When self-realisation comes, selfishness goes out. The two cannot stay together, even as light and darkness cannot dwell together.

Out of selfishness arises the sense of separateness from a fellow being. I feel that I am separate from you. Therefore, I must work for my own good, not thinking of your good. Now, if only I realise that you and I are one, there will be no selfishness.

There is a story of how the different limbs of the body got together. They said, "It is so unfair that, all the food is taken away by the stomach while we get nothing!" The hand said, "It is we who work but the food is taken away by the stomach." So they all struck work. When they went on a strike, no food was supplied to the stomach. Initially they felt very happy. They said, "Let the stomach understand." But eventually they found that they themselves became weak and emaciated in the process because it is only when the stomach gets food that energy is produced, blood is produced.

Likewise, we are all one. We are just different organs of the one universal body. Once we realise this, then there is no selfishness.

III. Frustration

How can you prevent frustration?

To prevent frustration we must first get to the root of the problem. What is the cause of frustration? The cause of frustration is a feeling of loneliness. It is only when man feels that he is all alone— there is no one by him— that he feels frustrated. Once he begins to realise that the Super Power, which, for want of a better word, we call God, is always by his side, there will be no frustration! Why is it, that the number of frustrated people is growing from day to day? Because people have turned away from God.

The answer to frustration is to turn back to God. Then you will never be frustrated at all.

How can we conquer frustration?

In your daily life, make God your senior partner. Hand yourself over in childlike trust to the Lord. The easiest way to conquer frustration is through self-surrender. We should come to God saying,

"Dear God, I come to you as I am. Accept me, make me, shape me, and mould me so that You are not ashamed of me." We should let go and let God take over. Invite God into your life.

God has two aspects—the mother aspect and the father aspect. I always think of God as my mother. If we appeal to the mother aspect of God, in a state of utter helplessness, we will get an immediate response. The words *"Jai, Jai, Jai, Jagadambaa"* are very powerful. But, don't say them just when you are entering a state of anger. Anger is temporary insanity and at that point, you won't remember these words. Instead, keep on repeating them throughout the day.

IV. Worry

If what is to happen must happen, why do we worry?

Yes, indeed, why do we worry? It is not enough to believe that what is to happen will happen. We need to go one step further. We need to believe that whatever happens, happens for the best. There is a meaning of mercy in every thing. All experiences in life come to teach us something. Don't look at the outer covering. Outer calamity is a fortune that comes to you in a soiled packet. Accept it and you will be abundantly blessed.

Can prayer overcome worry?

Prayer is the great bulwark against worry. How often do we lay waste our powers in worrying over things which have happened to us or which may—or as well may not—happen in the coming days! Every worry means a strain on our nerves. The more we worry, the more tense our nerves become, robbing us of our rest and peace of mind and heart. We then become easily agitated and excited. We quarrel without cause and become a nuisance to our near and dear ones!

Instead of worrying, let us learn to turn to God in prayer and place all our burdens at His Lotus Feet. This will give us an immediate feeling of relaxation and rest, enabling us to tackle the problems and perplexities of life in a spirit of calm surrender.

The man of prayer wonders at the spectacle of men and women carrying heavy loads on weak shoulders, when they can easily roll off the load at the feet of Him who alone is strong enough to bear all the burdens of all the worlds.

V. Criticism

Dada, I see faults in others. How can I avoid this?

In the measure in which I behold Sri Krishna in another, in that measure do I put my individual, personal, empirical self aside, and the Krishna in me deals with the Krishna in him. I no longer see his faults and frailties, his weaknesses and shortcomings. I penetrate through them and touch the Perfect One—the *Purushottama*—who sits and smiles in the hearts of all. I touch Him: He touches me, and the impossible happens! All jealousy and hatred depart. Misunderstandings cease, and enmity dies away. The world which is to many, a vale of tragedy and tears, becomes a garden of God!

People make mistakes—and this causes problems. How can we ignore them?

I urge you not to look at others' faults. By focusing attention on people's faults, you only draw negative forces to yourself. Moreover, fault-finding and magnifying others' mistakes are poor ways of changing the world.

A sunny temperament and a healthy sense of humour can do wonders for you. With a smile and a kind word, wrongs can be set right and wrong-doers set back on the right track.

VI. Hatred

Isn't hatred self-destructive?

Hatred was painted by an artist as an old man shrivelled up and pale as death, clutching in his claws lighted torches and serpents, and cruelly tearing out his heart with black decayed teeth. Asked to explain the significance of the picture, the artist said, "Hatred is an old man because it is as ancient as mankind, pale because he who hates, torments himself and lives a tragic life, with claws because it is so unmerciful, with torches and serpents because it creates discord, and it tears out its heart because it is self-destructive."

VII. Depression

What is the cause of depression?

The greatest killers of man are not heart attacks, cancer and accidents, but the clock, the calendar and the telephone. The price of financial success in modern times which is an age of tensions, is mounting everyday. The competitive spirit is cruel and ruthless, and drags many into depression.

Someone said, there are various types and causes of depression—tension, anxiety, competitive struggle, failure, frustration, disappointment in love, a guilty conscience.

How may we overcome depression?

To overcome depression,

1. We must never forget that depression is a temporary phase. Just as the sun goes into a sinking spell every night, but rises again the next morning, similarly depression is temporary. Affirm to yourself again and again, "This too shall pass away!"

2. Take care to see that your tensions do not accumulate.

ation
egoism. Violent
Seeker Service Silence Spirit
Vibrations Willpower Woman
Of The World Bhagavad G
Selfishness, Frustration, W
Rituals Sadhu Vaswani Sea
Thought Power Understanding
Education Faith Fear For
Meditation M

Therefore practise relaxation everyday and learn to take your troubles to God.

3. Find someone to whom you can unburden yourself. Understanding and patient listeners are needed.

4. Count your blessings.

VIII. Egoism

"I", "me" and "mine", the words we use most often, smell of egoism. How can we rise above them?

I think it is very difficult to overcome egoism on our own. Even as we become humble, this egoistic thought creeps into our minds, "I am so humble, and these people are so proud!" This is the pride of humility. When I regard myself as better than another, that is pride. When I regard myself as the lowliest of the low, that is humility, that is non-egoism.

There is a very beautiful incident described by the great Persian Sufi poet, Sadi. When Sadi was a young boy of six, his father, a *dervish*, took him to the mosque where a night long vigil was being observed. As the night grew, Sadi found that one after another, all the people who had assembled at the mosque, began to fall asleep. Only Sadi and his father remained awake. Even the *mullah* had nodded off. The little boy whispered into the ears of his father, "Father, only you and I are keeping the vigil. All the others have fallen asleep." His father admonished him, "It is better to go off to sleep and not observe the vigil, rather than find fault with others and think ourselves superior."

That is true humility. That is non-egoism, but not all of us can achieve it on our own. We need the grace of a *Guru* to do this, for egoism can take on very subtle forms and it becomes very difficult for

If you wish to be non-egoistic, you can begin by thinking, "All the others are better than I am, for there is something that I can learn from every human being."

The great Prophet of the Bahai faith, Baha'u'llah said to his disciples again and again, "If you find that there are nine vices and only one virtue in a man, forget the nine vices, and only think of his one virtue." This is the secret of true humility. See only the good in others. Then you will always feel that the others are better than you.

What is true humility?

No one reached God except on the path of humility. Humility, by revealing to us what we are, teaches us that of ourselves we can do nothing: for we are nothing. All the good that is done through us is done by God. Humility, therefore, means utter surrender to God and to God alone.

The best thing that man can do is to hand himself over to God, to accept everything including disgrace and disease, trouble and tribulation, misfortune and misery, as coming from God. Whatever comes from God is good. It cometh to purify. Therefore, rejoice in every situation and circumstance of life, giving gratitude to Him whose works are ever the works of mercy.

IX. Violent Dreams

Dear Dada, why do people get violent dreams?

I cannot give you a definite answer. The answer will differ from case to case. But the general answer is that the reason why we get violent dreams is that we spend our entire day in stress and tension. All that stress and tension accumulates in the subconscious self. And the subconscious self throws it out at night in the form of dreams. We watch the TV for hours together and there are so many scenes of violence which we see. All that enters the subconscious. We must be very careful about every thing that we watch, about everything that we hear, about everything that we read, about everything that we take in. If all these things get stored up in the subconscious, it will definitely throw it out in the form of dreams.

If you do not want nightmares, or violent dreams, one very good thing that will help you is this, as you are about to slip into sleep, carry with yourself a line from the sayings of a great one, a saint of God, a *satpurkha*, some benefactor of humanity. Repeat those words over and over again as you slip into the realm of sleep. Or take with yourself the gracious form of your *gurudeva*, your *Ishtadeva*. Feel that you are sitting in His lap. And you will be blessed with wonderful dreams. In those dreams, the great masters will come to you and reveal to you truths which books cannot explain.

X. Loneliness

How may we overcome loneliness?

Loneliness has become a major problem in many cities all over the world. An ever-increasing number of people feel that life has no meaning and is not worth living.

There are three types of loneliness—there is the loneliness of isolation, alienation and separation. The way to overcome loneliness is to realise that God and man are comrades in the endless adventure of existence.

Give us some practical steps to tackle this problem.

1. Develop constant awareness of God by reminding yourself, again and again, of the truth that you are not alone, God is with

2. Never forget to keep your daily appointment with God. Everyday, preferably at the same time and place, sit in silence and pray, meditate or do your spiritual thinking.

3. Man's extremity is God's opportunity. If you have a difficult problem—of health, personal relation, finance, etc.— hand it over to God. In God is the solution to every problem.

4. Keep on shooting brief prayers to God.

5. Help others. In the measure in which you go out of yourself and help others, in that measure you will overcome loneliness. You will realise that you are not apart from others. You and the others are parts of One whole.

Parents and Children

There is no friendship, no love, like that of the parent for the child.
— Henry Ward Beecher

You are busy gathering silver and gold but you have neglected your richest treasure. Your richest treasure is your children.
— Sadhu Vaswani

How should parents raise their children?

By love and patience, proper guidance and discipline. Without discipline, no art can be learnt and, most of all, the art of living.

Today, the cult of self-expression is abroad. I am told we have imported it from America. I hear the people say, "Don't restrain your children. Don't discipline them. Let them express themselves freely." But what "self" is it that seeks expression and defies all rules of discipline? Surely, it is not the higher self of man. It is the lower self, the ego—the self of desires and unruly passions, of cravings and animal appetites. When man surrenders to the lower self, he behaves no better than a brute beast.

I read a headline which appeared in an American newspaper, "School gang violence near-epidemic: Vandalism, murder, arson, burglary." And the paper quoted a member of the Los Angeles County Board of Supervisors as saying, "We are going to have to return to discipline. Without discipline in the home, we are not going to have it in the schools or in the streets. We must arouse public opinion for a change." The paper also reported how three teenagers—aged fourteen, fifteen, and seventeen—had killed a woman and a man just to steal from them three dollars and ten dollars respectively. India, beware!

Discipline is necessary. But discipline must not be confounded with suppression. There was a little boy who, asked what his name was, answered, "Haresh don't!" Everytime he wanted to do something, his parents said to him, "Haresh, don't!" That is not true discipline. We must train our children by explaining to them the purpose of life and teach them the rules and discipline needed to reach life's goals.

Our mothers taught us through precept and examples. They told us wonderful stories from the ancient scriptures. They were careful to indicate how life might be lived in the right way, by devoting our energies to the service of certain high ideals. The scriptural stories, learnt in the years of childhood and boyhood, leave an indelible impression upon young minds.

And discipline must be blended with love, so that the child has the assurance that he is not alone, that there is someone who cares for him, and to whom he can turn, at any time of the day or night.

I believe what the children need is time, attention and love. Without love, no child can grow in the right way. Today parents are busy doing many things, but they have neglected the one thing needful— being examples before their children. The child learns more through example than preaching.

Can you offer some practical suggestions to parents desirous of bringing up their children in the right way?

Here are a few tips which may be found helpful:

1. There is a difference between children and adults. Children live in the now; they are free from anxieties of the past and fear of the future. If a child is in need of something or wants an answer to a question, never say to him, "I shall fulfil your need or answer your question tomorrow or at my leisure."

There is a story about a young man, the son of a famous writer, who was sent to jail and whom the judge admonished, saying, "You should be ashamed of yourself. Your father is such a great man!" Without hesitation, the young man retorted, "It is true, my father is a great man. He is always busy with his writing work. Each time I went to him with a question, he said to me, "Not now, my child, I haven't the time to answer your question. Come tomorrow!"

2. Every child is a human being, with a heart and soul. Never let him feel unwanted. And never forget that the child is an individual, with his own personality and innate talents. Understand him and encourage the creative principle within him to express itself freely. Guide him in a healthy, constructive way by bringing out the best that is in him. Do not impose your will on him and say, "I am a doctor, so my son should become a doctor!"

3. In your treatment towards children, do not discriminate. Do not let them feel that a particular child is your favourite. Children are very sensitive creatures.

4. Keep your child very close to yourself, until he is at least three years of age. He needs your affectionate touch. It is a great blunder to hand over little children to *ayahs* or baby-sitters.

5. It sometimes becomes very necessary to scold children. Whenever you do so, avoid being emotional. Let your words on such occasions be like whips of love. Explain the fault clearly to the child, and allow him to speak out, if he has anything to say.

6. Even at a young age, children should be trained to attend to household chores. Let them cultivate reverence for manual work.

7. Let children grow in a spirit of unselfishness by training them to share food with the starving ones. Sri Krishna says in the Gita, "He who cooks for himself alone, is a thief!" Before you eat your food, set apart a share for a hungry one— a man, a bird, or an animal. Example is always a better teacher than precept.

8. The home is a door to the kingdom of God, the kingdom of true happiness. Let all the members of the family gather together,

at an appointed time everyday, at a prayer meeting— even if it be for ten to fifteen minutes. This will give a new tone to the home. At a prominent place in your home, keep a big, beautiful picture of some great one— Krishna or Rama, Buddha or Jesus, Zoroaster or Guru Nanak, Mira or Mahavir, Baha'u'llah or Kabir or a saint or a saviour of humanity— to whom you feel drawn. Whenever you or the children leave the house or enter it, bow down to the picture and offer a small prayer.

In families today, parents discipline their children by scolding them and punishing them. They use expressions like, "Bad behaviour, bad girl, bad boy" in the hope of changing their behaviour. Is there an alternative?

The alternative is that we must give more time and more attention to our children. And we must give them the pure, selfless love of the heart. We have denied these three things to our children. The truth of the matter is that no child can grow in the right way without love. Today, for the sake of convenience, we have handed the children over to the TV screen. The TV shows them many good things that they should see, but also things they should not see.

Interestingly, it takes longer for the good things to have an effect on the mind of the child, while negative things have a quicker effect on the child. Parents today are busy making money. When I ask them, "Why are you making money?" They answer, "We are making money for our children." But, in the bargain, they lose their children because they don't give them time, attention, or the love of their hearts.

Are parents to be blamed for neglecting their children?

Not many parents seem to realise their responsibilities towards the children. It was William Tame who said, "Men are generally more careful about the breed of their horses and dogs than their own children."

Of Plato, the great Greek philosopher, it is said that when he found a child doing wrong, he went and corrected the father for it.

Do fathers have a role to play in bringing up children?

Fathers usually feel that they have no share of responsibility in bringing up their children in the right way. They believe that it is the mother's job. They come and go in the house as boarders with no active interest in the welfare of their children. They treat demands of business as the cause of their neglect. It must not be forgotten that no amount of piling of the earth's treasure can compensate a man for the loss of his incomparable jewels— his children.

A father was a member of several clubs and associations with the result that he always returned home late in the night. He could not be at home even for a single evening. He was away in the morning before the children were up and returned late when the children were asleep. Even on Sundays, he was not at home. He had to attend meetings of associations of which he was a member. The children pined for their father's company, until they had an idea. They formed a family association and, of course, named the father as the president. Now he had to stay home at least one evening in a week, to preside over the non-political, domestic group.

Dadaji, how could we make the generation gap a pleasant experience?

The difficulty with the young people, and I too regard myself as one of them, is that we think that we have mastered the knowledge and wisdom of the whole world. We carry it on the palm of our hands. If only we realise that our parents have passed through many experiences and gathered wisdom from which we can learn, this generation gap will not be a problem. It is because the children feel that their parents don't understand them and do not know anything, that the generation gap is created.

I believe, it is the duty of the parents to become friends with their children when they are in their teens. In their teens, young boys and girls need friends more than parents. The parent must become a friend so that the teenager comes and confides everything in the parents.

In our days, there was no generation gap at all. We never heard the word, generation gap. We hear of it now. Why? Because in our days, all of the mother's time, her energies, her attention, were devoted to the upbringing of the children. Today, so many mothers have to go and earn. They are absent from the house for many hours at a stretch. Or those who do not have the necessity to earn, go to clubs. They neglect their children which creates this generation gap.

In our days, there was no generation gap. And no one taught us not to smoke, not to eat meat, not to drink wine! We were brought up in that atmosphere, therefore, it became natural for us. Till today I have never smoked! It was not because I was told not to smoke but because we were in that atmosphere.

The best discipline is self-discipline. Unless you have self-discipline, unless you have self-control, you cannot lead a disciplined life.

The father says to the boy, "You must not smoke," but he himself turns round and smokes. The boy sees the father smoking and says, "He tells me not to smoke and he is enjoying himself. I will also enjoy myself." The boy also turns round and starts smoking. Examples speak louder than words.

Dadaji, what is the difference between today's generation and yesterday's generation?

The difference between today's generation and yesterday's generation is only the difference that is between today and yesterday. Your question contains the answer. But if you ask me, what is it that today's generation needs? I will give the answer in one word— reverence, which is the root of knowledge. Without reverence, there can be no true education, there can be no true knowledge.

That is why the great English poet said, "Let knowledge grow from more to more, but more of reverence in us dwell." We are becoming more and more irreverent today. Yesterday's generation had greater reverence for their parents, their elders, their teachers and for the one indefinable mystery, which, for want of a better word, we call, God.

Reverence is of three types. Reverence for what is above us, reverence for what is around us and what is beneath us. Reverence for the poor, the broken ones, the blind, the handicapped, the naive, and reverence for birds and animals, who, too, are our brothers and sisters in the one family of creation. If only this reverence could enter our hearts, the world would become new.

Respected Dada, my mother is very particular about Indian values, rituals and culture, and tries to influence me to accept the same. Sometimes, I find it very hard to do so, growing up here in Manila. I know my mom means good for me, but at this point, what can I do to improve? I am a first year college student.

Values need to be engraved, when you are little children. The process must start from that time onwards. It is believed, that values are engraved in the pre-natal period, even before you are born, while you are in the mother's womb. If your mother has not been able to do so, if she is asking you to respect those values after you have grown up, I can understand it must be difficult for you to adjust yourself.

Values, I believe, need to be engraved when you are little children. I think it is the duty of mothers to start training you and teaching you those values right from the period when you are children, then there will be no conflict in your mind.

In the West, we find children drifting away from parents. Is there a way in which family life can be kept intact? And what may we do to inculcate among the minds of children, born in the West, love for Indian culture and tradition?

In the West, I find people are busy amassing wealth. Alas, they neglect their richest treasure! Our richest treasure is our children.

I would place the following five-point programme before the parents:

1. Everyday, all the members of the family— from the youngest to the eldest— should spend a little time in prayer together. The family that prays together, stays together. At such sessions, a thought from a scripture or an inspirational book should be read, and each and every member should be asked to offer his or her reflection on the thought. This will give them a sense of involvement.

2. The mother is the greatest influence in the life of a child, especially during the formative years, when he is best mouldable and impressionable. She should be a model for the children to follow, for it is in the home that habits are formed and character is made. The mother, by the shining example of her life, can infuse in the children, love for Indian tradition and culture, so that the

children know where their roots are. Therefore it is incumbent that the mothers themselves are well versed in the Indian tradition.

3. The father has also an important part to play. In spite of his pre-occupations, he must spend, everyday, as much time as possible with his children. In any case, he could take the family out on weekends and go out on a small holiday somewhere, at least once in every six months.

4. The TV has come to occupy a dominant place in the house. In all their free time, the children's eyes are glued to the TV screens. This has a harmful effect on their eyes, and the impact made by undesirable elements shown on the TV is indelible. Substitute the TV by some healthy and creative pastime for the children.

5. Start weekly classes for the children where they could be introduced to and taught the essentials of India's deathless culture. Such groups, if desired may be named, "I belong to India" groups, so that the children realise, that although they stay in a land so far away from their homeland, they yet belong to India, and feel proud about being inheritors of a rich, immortal culture and tradition, which is regarded as the hope of the world.

Dada, why don't parents allow their children to date?

Let me answer your question by telling you a conversation I heard between a girl and her mother.

The girl asked her mother, "Mummy, may I go out this evening with my boy friend?"

"No, my child", said the mother.

"Why mummy, don't you trust me?"

geism, Violent Silence Spirit
eeker Service Silence Spirit Willpower Woman
Vibrations Of The World Bhagavad G
Selfishness, Frustration
Rituals Sadhu Vaswani Se
Thought-Power Understanding
Education Faith Four Forg
Meditation Mi
And G

"I do trust you, my child," said the mother.

"Then, don't you trust my boy friend?"

"I do trust him," the mother said.

"Then what is the reason?" asked the girl.

And the mother said, "I don't trust the two of you together!"

How can we inculcate faith in our children?

To enhance the faith of children, it is essential, that we narrate to them stories of God, *avataras*, saints and spiritual leaders. This will make them aware that there is a great *shakti* which is moving the entire universe.

We should also keep an eye on their company. It would be a good thing to take them to the *satsang*; if this is not possible, arrange a small *satsang* in your own home; have lamps lit, and do *aarti*; at the end of the *aarti*, let the children be given some *prasad*.

From time to time, arrange a service programme in which the children can participate. Let them develop the spirit of compassion for the poor, the lonely and the downtrodden.

Children are the builders of the future. They are our greatest treasure. Therefore, let us give them a healthy, happy, harmonious atmosphere at home. Let us impart such an education to them that the seeds of faith, courage, piety, compassion and strength of character, may be sown in their hearts.

How do we accept our parents' views when ours are different? Sometimes we cannot agree. What do we do?

There is a great man who has said, "When I was 20, I felt that my parents were foolish. I knew everything. They knew nothing. At the age of 30, I began to see that there was some little wisdom in what my parents said. At the age of 40, I found that there was not a little, but quite a lot of wisdom in what they said. At the age of 50, I have realised that I was a fool to have disregarded what my parents told me."

It is true that there are many points on which youths disagree with adults, especially in this period, which is a transitional period. Values are changing. The values of those that are advanced in age are different from the values of those that are just entering into these experiences of life.

One thing I think that can help, is to put yourself in the place of your parents. I do not ask you to accept everything that the parents tell you because, may be, from your point of view, the parents do not understand the problems you face. But you must try to put yourself in the place of your parents and consider what your condition would be if your children behaved towards you, as you are behaving towards your parents.

Second, the parents should grow in patience. I tell parents, again and again, that you should be a friend, to your children. You must be so easily accessible to them and so very understanding in regard to their problems that they do not hesitate in telling you everything. What happens now is that the children try to hide many things from their parents, which is wrong. That is what is going to cut at the very roots of family life.

When a child grows to be a teenager, parents have to become friends of their children. The attitude alike of parents and children needs to be changed. Children should be more respectful to their parents. Parents should be more understanding in regard to the problems that the children have to face. It is only then, that we will be able to build up family life once again. As it is, the gulf between children and parents is widening.

Thirdly, also try to explain to yourself that your parents have already similar problems when they were children and it is through, their experiences that they want to give you the right type of advice. Listen to them. Think over what they tell you and then do what you think is right.

Why are mothers always right?

It is only for the sake of expediency that mothers are always right. Not from the absolute point of view. I went to an office. On each one of the desks at which the workers sat, there was a small placard on which were written the words, "The boss is always right."

I do not think that is correct in a family. In an industrial organisation, it can be right. If I think the boss is not right, I can leave the organisation and go and join another. But a family is a family, you cannot leave it and join another family. There should always be a give-and-take arrangement.

Dadaji, inspite of guidance, advice and suggestions from parents, why is it that youngsters today do not follow the path of truth sincerely?

Why? It is for the young people to answer. That is the question you must answer. One of the reasons perhaps is that whatever is told to them, they do not take seriously.

Another reason is because the parents themselves, do not bear witness in deeds of daily living, to the teachings they would wish to pass on to their children. A parent should be a model of the teaching that he wishes to pass on. The child learns not through words, but through life.

What type of life are the parents living? If the mother and the father are quarrelling with each other all the time, and if they tell the child never to quarrel with anyone, how can the child understand?

There was a little child. The father said to him, "You must never speak an untruth." The boy said, "Yes, daddy. It is a wonderful teaching you have given me. I shall try to abide by it. I shall never speak an untruth." And the child really attempted to be true to that ideal.

One day, a man came and knocked at the door. The child opened the door. "Is your father inside?" asked the man. "Kindly wait, I will go and see if he is inside," said the child. He went to the father's bedroom, found that the father was there and told him that a man had come to meet him. "Tell him that daddy is not at home," said the father. Now this little boy had to speak the truth. So he came out and said to the man, "Sir, daddy says that I must tell you that he is not at home."

If you have this type of duplicity, what is the child going to do? That is the great difficulty. Our elders place before us ideals to which their lives, their deeds of daily living, do not bear witness. And they feel disillusioned.

How can we develop friendship with our children ?

To develop friendship with your children you must:

1. Start early. Don't wait until they become teenagers. Then it will be too late.

2. The first time your children meet you in the morning or when they return from school, greet them warmly. Press their arm, give them a hug or a kiss to assure them that they are important to you.

3. Develop close proximity with your children till they are three years old. At that tender age, they need your affectionate touch and your warm response to everything they do or say.

4. Be a good listener. When the child is talking to you, give him your full attention. Do not dismiss him summarily. Listen to him patiently. Every child wants an interested ear.

5. Try to understand your child. No child expects his parents to agree with him all the time, but he has a right to be understood.

6. Do not humiliate your children, especially in the presence of their peers.

7. Don't let down the trust of a child especially if he trusts you with a secret, regard it as sacred.

8. To deal with your children in the right way, you need to cultivate a rich sense of humour.

9. Meal times should be times of coming closer to each other. The TV should be switched off.

10. If you want to make friends with your children, you must know their friends.

11. Do not discriminate among children. Let them not have a feeling that one of them is your favourite.

12. Children should be encouraged to help with domestic chores, especially at an early age. This gives them a sense of belonging, a sense of contribution to the family.

13. Don't create fantasies about your child's future according to your own expectations and desires. We must not regard our children as an extension of our hopes and dreams.

14. Encourage the children to share food with the starving ones— human beings, birds and animals.

15. Remember, a home is a door to the Kingdom of God. Everyday, at an appointed hour, all the members of the family, young and old, must get together at a prayer meeting. This will create a new atmosphere of love and harmony and peace in the house. The family that prays together, stays together.

Is it necessary for a mother to feed a new born child?

There are many mothers today, who do not want to breast-feed their children. Sometimes, it occurs to me that perhaps the growing incidence of breast cancer can be traced to this cause. The milk that is produced in the mother's breast is the property of the infant. It is neither the property of the mother nor of the father. The mother who refrains from giving the milk to the child is actually stealing what belongs to the infant.

Nature has no judges, no courts, no policemen to arrest you for any wrong that you may do. Nature works in a simple way and it has its own methods of punishing us for our wrong doing. In this case, nature reacts by creating cancer in the breasts.

It has been seen that children who receive milk from their mother's breasts, are the ones who love and revere their parents. And those children easily live in accordance with the ideals placed before them by their parents.

Peace of Mind

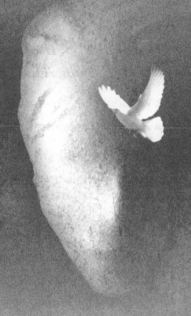

A person who is not disturbed by the incessant flow of desires can alone achieve peace and not the man who strives to satisfy such desires.
— Bhagavad Gita

God takes life's broken pieces and gives us unbroken peace.
— Wilburt Donald Gouch

What is peace?

Like love, peace is to be felt. I may tell you what peace is in many words, but you will not understand those words until you yourself have felt peace in the heart within.

Dadaji, while playing the part that one has been given in this birth, one comes across many upsetting incidents. How can we forget an upsetting incident and maintain inner equilibrium?

We feel upset because we get attached. That is the difficulty. If I do my work as though I am playing a part, I would not be upset.

Another way to face upsetting situations is to say, as Sadhu Vaswani used to say, "God upsets our plans to set up His own. And His plans are always perfect."

If we have the faith that whatever has happened to me is according to the plan of the Highest; that there is some hidden good in it for me, I will not be upset. Sadhu Vaswani also used to say, "Every disappointment is His appointment. And He knows best."

In the second chapter of the *Bhagavad Gita*, the Lord gives us a wonderful picture in a few *slokas*. These *slokas* were very dear to the heart of Mahatma Gandhi. He had them recited, I am told, everyday, at his prayer meetings. They are *slokas* concerning what the Lord calls, *sthita prajana*, the balanced man. The man who will not be upset by anything that may happen. He knows that it is all a play.

If something happens in a play, do you feel upset? Supposing somebody comes and scolds you, speaks ill of you in a play, you don't feel upset, do you? You know that the part is to be played out. If only you do this one thing— that is, remember all the time that you are an actor, the real you is something different, you have been made to play this part in this particular life— you will not get entangled.

In this play, you have to play a double role. You have to be an actor on the one hand and a spectator on the other. You have to watch the play and you also have to act. If you do this, you will not lose your peace of mind.

Dada, how does one attain peace of mind, especially when there is so much stress and tension?

There is truly one way of achieving peace of mind. And that is the way of self-realisation. Once you realise yourself, there is no more tension no more stress. You abide in a state of tranquillity and peace. You may not be able to achieve it, overnight. It is a process through which you have to move.

Therefore, one very easy way of attaining peace of mind, is to sit in silence everyday for 10 to 15 minutes and explain to yourself this one thing— that whatever happens, happens according to the Will of God.

Why is it that we lose our peace of mind? Because our wishes, our desires are crossed. I want a particular thing to be done in a particular manner, it has happened in an opposite manner, my peace is disturbed.

A girl met me this afternoon. She said, "I don't want my child to cry but the child keeps on crying all the time. That disturbs my peace." Then I asked her, "Were you a child at any time?" She said, "Of course, I was a child only 20 years ago." I asked, "Did you ever cry?" "Of course I cried," came the reply. Then I asked, "Why don't you permit your child to cry? You cried and you don't permit your child to cry!"

We must understand, that whatever happens, happens according to the Will of God. This, which has happened contrary to my wishes, contrary to my desires, has happened according to God's Will. There must be some good in it for me.

Explain this to your mind everyday, "O mind, why is it that you lose your peace? You lose your peace, because your wishes are not fulfilled. But above your wishes is the Will of God. Accept His Will and you will never lose your peace."

What is the easiest way for a common man to remain calm in the midst of trying circumstances?

You will get peace of mind if you give your own "piece" to others. The great saint, Sant Tulsidas, says: *"Tulsi is sansar mein kar leejye do kaam, dene ko tukra bhala, lene ko Hari naam."* He says, keep on giving. When you have learnt to give, you have learnt to live aright. Then peace automatically wakes up in the heart within. It is only because we are so selfish that our peace is disturbed. Peace is our original nature. We are built of peace.

What is it that has disturbed our peace? Sordid selfishness. We have to overcome this selfishness, only then can we return to our original state. Each one of us is *sat chit ananda. Ananda* is the peace that can never be disturbed. *Ananda* is the joy, the bliss that no ending knows. We have only to get back to our original state.

You must have seen on several occasions when your mind is terribly disturbed and you go and do a little painting, you find that you have become peaceful suddenly. Why? Because you forgot yourself in this creative work. Likewise, when we move out of ourselves and give joy to those who are in need of joy, we forget ourselves.

All we need to do is to forget ourselves and peace will be ours. When we forget this outer self, we draw closer to the real, the inner self which is peace.

ation Life
geism. Violent Dream Spiritual
Seeker Service Silence Spiritual
Realisations Willpower Woman Yoga
Of The World Bhagavad Gita G
Selfishness, Frustration, Worry
Rituals Sadhu Vaswani Science
Thought Power Understanding
Education Faith Fear For
Meditation M
And C

Is it possible to lead a life of bliss in this troubled world?

It is not only possible but your birthright. *Anandam* is your birthright as children of God. Each one of you is a son or a daughter of God. And God is the Source of *Ananda*. He is an unending Source of bliss. The moment I realise that I am a child of God, nothing is going to affect me. In order to live a life of bliss, all we have to do is to transcend the phenomenal, transcend what is happening around us.

Living in this materialistic world, how may we attain peace?

We live in an economy of war and yet affirm that we want peace. Our industrial economy creates demands. The enticing advertisements on the TV screen and in the newspapers awaken desires within the heart of man. Everyone wants more and more— more comforts, pleasures, luxuries, possessions, wealth, a more convenient life-style. Many of our desires remain unfulfilled, and that leads to frustration. The great teachers of India have taught that simple living and high thinking leads to fulfilment and freedom.

God loves each one of us with a love which is immeasurable. He has given us the most perfect machine— the human body— and the most perfect computer— the human brain. Let us not forget that every breath is valuable and must be spent in worthwhile pursuits. Let us set aside a portion of our daily food for a hungry one— a man, a bird, an animal. Let us speak the truth, kindly and softly and do all we can, to help as many as we can, to lift the load on the rough road of life. That is the way to peace.

Prayer

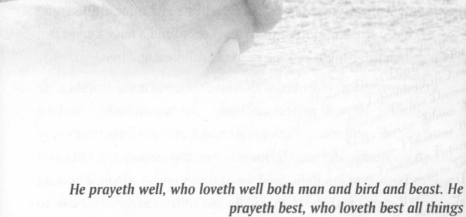

He prayeth well, who loveth well both man and bird and beast. He prayeth best, who loveth best all things both great and small.
— Samuel Taylor Coleridge

You pray in your distress and in your need; would that you might pray also in the fullness of your joy and in your days of abundance.
— Kahlil Gibran

ration Lip
goism. Violent Dre... Spiritu...
Seeker Service Silence Will power Woman of ... Science
... Of The World Bhagavad Ga... Understanding
... Selfishness, Frustration. Wo... Faith Fear For
... Rituals Sadhu Vaswani Thought... Education... Meditation M
... And...

You have always said that we should pray. But how do we really pray?

Prayer is not a difficult matter. It is like meeting a friend. Suppose a friend were to come to you. It would be so natural for you to discuss with him your life, your dreams, perplexities, aspirations, and desires. Do likewise with God. He is the One Friend of all friends. When all other friends fade away, He is the one friend who will remain. But the difficulty is, how to get in touch with Him? Therefore, you must believe firstly, that God is all around you. You do not have to go to a particular place to meet Him. It is always good to go to temples, shrines, churches, mosques. But you do not have to go to a particular place to be able to contact Him. He is right in front of you. All you have to do is to close your eyes, shut out the world, open your heart, call Him with deep love and longing and there He is in front of you. You may cultivate some type of relationship with God. Tell God— you are my father, my mother, my brother, my friend, you are the beloved of my heart and everyday, try to strengthen the relationship you have cultivated with God.

If there is a person without faith who is not inclined towards prayer, can we still urge him to pray? Would it be a mockery if he repeated mere words without sincerity?

I don't think that by urging others to pray, they will be led on the path of prayer. Prayer is something that comes from within. Until a person has arrived at that stage, he will not be able to relish prayer. It is like a person who is sick: he does not relish good food.

Then, how do we go about helping him?

We can pray for him. We can ask God to so bless him that he may be brought on the path of prayer. But there are agnostics. Who say that they do not know if there is a God. To such a one, we can recommend the prayer. 'If Thou art, do thou listen to me,' so that he makes no commitment. That is a start for an agnostic. But for an atheist, we need to pray, so that he is brought to the path of prayer, so that faith may awaken within him.

Each one of us is essentially a divine spark. That divine spark is veiled within many veils. Those veils have to be rent asunder. There, prayer can help. Once the divinity within a man is awakened, his prayer becomes natural.

If a man who is suffering a lot and is unhappy prays, and confines his prayers only to the praise of the Lord without asking for anything, wouldn't that be the highest form of prayer?

Yes, that would indeed be the highest form of prayer provided he is able to do so. He will be able to do it only when he has arrived at that level, when he realises the vanity, the emptiness of all that the world is seeking, when he realises that the only true blessing of life is God Himself.

There was once a very poor man. From the worldly point of view, he wanted everything. But his one constant prayer was, "God, people come to Thee to ask of Thee so many things. I need nothing else but Thee. Give me the alms of Thy love. That's all I want."

There was another, whose prayer was, "God, I ask of Thee only one thing. The gift of Thyself."

Such prayers come out of a heart which are a very high level. Most of us are like children in the kindergarten class.

Even when our prayer is a petition, is it acceptable to God?

All God wants of us is that we go to Him. In the measure in which we think of approaching Him, our level of consciousness rises. This is the beauty of a life of prayer. Start with praying for whatever you desire. You will find, that in the bargain, your level of consciousness will keep on rising.

Should we not feel ashamed to ask God for petty things?

No, not at all. The option is either to ask worldly people or to go directly to God, who is our father, our mother, our true parent. Why must we hesitate in asking anything from our father or mother? To whom else will a child turn?

A stage comes when we realise that what we are asking for is not worth having— therefore we begin to ask for what is really worth having, which is the Lord Himself.

Can we ask God to help us in gambling?

Through gambling, prayer will take us to a stage of non-gambling. Supposing I go to God and ask for a particular horse to win, and it so happens that the horse does win, I will get drawn to God and a stage will come when I will realise the falsity of gambling.

God answers our prayers in three ways. To some of our prayers He says— yes, my child. What you ask for is good for you and I will grant it. To some other prayers, He says— no, my child. What you are asking for is not the right thing for you; therefore I will not grant it. His third answer is— wait. I will give you what you want, but the time has not yet come. Yes, no, and wait— these are the three answers.

There are those who ask for favours and offer to do certain acts of abstinence or make sacrifices, or give charity in return. What of this bartering or even bribing? Is this form of making deals with God, improper?

It may not appear to be proper when you look at it from that higher point of view. But I believe that whatever contact we have with God, will ultimately take us to God.

There are thieves who, before they go to steal, visit a temple and promise God a share of the loot. From every point of view, this is absolutely wrong. But, their very act of going to God makes them think of God and so is good for them. Who knows, one day their soul will wake up, and they will keep away from their sinful activity. Each time they think of God, their inner instrument (*antahkarana*) will be purified. It is the stage of inner purification that leads to illumination.

There are three stages on the mystic path. The first is inner purification. The second is illumination. The third is unification. In the stage in which most of us are, we need purification.

How can we judge or measure our own state of inner purification?

We cannot. There is no yardstick to judge your own spiritual progress. You will find that as you progress spiritually, you become more kind, more loving, more gentle, and more soft-spoken. Although not a gauge, these qualities indicate that we are moving along the path of inner purification.

As we move closer and closer to the Lotus Feet of the Lord, we realise that we ourselves are nothing. It is all His grace, His love, His mercy.

By myself, I can do nothing. That is the very first principle of spiritual life. The second principle is—He that is within you is greater than he that is outside. All these external forces, appear to be tremendous, and strong. But they are nothing compared to that which is within you— the Lord, who is seated on the throne of your heart.

Ideally, what should be the concept of God?

God is beyond all concepts because God cannot be reached with the help of the senses or with the help of the mind. God transcends both the senses and the mind.

Is there a distinction between prayer and meditation? How do they relate to one another? Do both practices imply communion with God?

Prayer can go on for twenty-four hours, meditation cannot.

There is one essential difference between prayer and meditation. You can pray and still be doing the humdrum things of life. You can be doing your work and the prayers go on. You cannot do that in meditation. Meditation is a process of withdrawal. A prayer does not involve that state of withdrawal. Prayer is living in the world and still communing with God. Meditation is withdrawing from the world and communing with God.

What is the relation between work and worship? For instance, it is time for prayer and at the same time duty is to be performed to please one's parents. Which is more important?

The relationship between work and worship is that work should be done in a spirit of worship, and when we worship, we must not neglect our work.

One of the most important words expressed by the Lord in the *Bhagavad Gita* is *swadharma*. Each one of us has his own obligations to fulfill. My duties are not your duties. Your duties are not my duties. The father has his own duty, the mother has hers, the children have theirs, the teacher has his, the students have theirs, the employers have their duties, and the employees have their duties. Each one must be true to the duty that belongs to him. You must never, never neglect your duty. But the Lord says, after doing your duty, you must find some time, come and sit in a silent corner and do your spiritual thinking. Sit in a silent corner, pray, meditate, repeat the Name divine, engage yourself in a loving and intimate conversation with God. But you must not attend to worship and ignore your duty.

When you talk about work and worship, I am reminded of the story of Pundalik. Pundalik was such a great devotee of the Lord, that the Lord Himself came down to earth to have his *darshan* once. Just imagine, Sri Krishna standing at the doorstep, asking to have a *darshana* of His devotee. At that time, Pundalik was giving a bath to his dear parents who were too old and weak to look after themselves. Seeing Sri Krishna at the door, Pundalik throws a brick at him, saying, "Lord, please stand on this brick and wait while I attend to my parents."

What did the Lord do? He was not angry; He did not feel insulted. He just stood on the brick and waited patiently, while His humble devotee bathed his parents.

Here is a shining example of *swadharma* for you. The Lord who stood on the brick is known in Maharashtra as *Vithoba*— the standing one, He who stood on the brick and waited for the sake of his devotee who was fulfilling his duty by his parents.

Which is the best time for prayer? And the best place?

It is commonly supposed that the best time for prayer is either the silent hour of the dawn or the sacred hour of evening twilight, and that the best place for prayer is some quiet nook or some silent spot on a river bank, in a forest grove, or on a mountain-peak. But there can be no better time for prayer than now and no better place than wherever we happen to be. To grow in the spirit of prayer, we must realise that the circumstances in which we are placed are the very best for us at any given time.

Dada, do we need to know a theory of prayer?

As a college student, I was a member of a small group called the "prayer circle". We met together every evening and studied some

geism Violent
Seeker Service Silence Spir
Vibrations Willpower Woman Bo
Of The World Bhagavad G
Selfishness Frustration
Rituals Sadhu Vaswani Sec
Thought Power Education Faith Fear Forc
Understanding
Meditation At
And

treatise on prayer by some leading authority on the subject. It was a highly interesting study. I learnt so much about "types" and "levels" and "degrees" of prayer, about "low" and "middle" and "high" prayer, about the difference between prayer and meditation and contemplation, and about many other things. I became almost an "authority" myself on the theory of prayer. But to my deep consternation, I found that whereas, prior to my studies in prayer, I could pray so easily, so naturally, so spontaneously, I could no longer do so, in spite of my extensive knowledge of the theory of prayer.

I left off going to the "prayer circle". And it took me long to unlearn what I had learnt, and to get back to my original state of simplicity, when I could, in prayer, speak to God as a child to its mother.

To be able to pray, you need not know— I would even say, you should not know— the theory of prayer. I know of several who have read and mastered difficult books on prayer–some of who, indeed, have written books and lectured on prayer— but who, alas, do not know how to pray!

Dada, do we have to be well versed in the Scriptures, in order to pray effectively?

You don't have to be learned or highly educated to be able to pray. Indeed, too much learning or education, far from being a help, becomes a hindrance in the way of prayer. Sri Ramakrishna was illiterate: he could not sign his name. Yet he prayed for hours together. He prayed as one who stood in the presence of God, speaking to Him, as a servant to his master, as a friend to his friend, as a child to its mother. "Have you seen God?" he was asked. And he answered, "Yes, more clearly than I see you!"

Education is not needed. Knowledge of books is not needed, wealth is not needed: a separate prayer room is not needed, physical strength is not needed. What is needed is a loving heart eager to wait upon God.

Art, music, scriptural lore, rituals and ceremonies are not needed. What is needed is a heart contrite and lowly, pure and holy— a loving heart eager to wait upon God.

Is it necessary to memorise our prayers?

Prayer is waiting upon God— in love and longing. Without this, repetition of set prayers becomes vain. So often, prayers are read from books. They do good in so far as they draw our attention to God. Mere mechanical repetition is a waste of time.

Dada, you often speak of the power of prayer. Please elaborate.

Today, a number of scientists bear testimony to the power of prayer. The world famous Nobel Laureate, Dr. Alexis Carrel wrote, "Prayer is the most powerful form of energy that one can generate." He also wrote, "Prayer is a force as real as terrestrial gravity. I have seen men, after all other therapies had failed, lifted out of disease and melancholy by the serene effect of prayer... the world, today, stands on the edge of destruction. Why? Because the people have forgotten to pray. Our deepest source of power and perfection has been left miserably underdeveloped."

Bobson, the great statistician of our century, wrote, "The greatest undeveloped resource of the world is faith and the greatest unused power is prayer."

Pierre Curie (husband of Marie Curie) was another Nobel Laureate in science. One day, he was in his laboratory, stooping over a microscope. A student entered. Not noticing the microscope, he

ation Le
goism, Violent D..
Seeker Service Silence Spirit
celebrations Willpower Woman L
Of The World Bhagavad G
Selfishness, Frustration, W
Rituals Sadhu Vaswani Se
Thought-Power Understanding
Education Faith Fear For
Meditation M
And C

thought that the scientist was offering a prayer. He began tip-toeing out of the laboratory. Pierre Curie called him back.

"I thought you were praying, sir," said the student.

"I was, son," said the scientist with his usual simplicity and again turned to the microscope.

He then added, "All science, research and study, is a prayer— a prayer that God will reveal His eternal secrets to us. For God does have secrets which He reveals only when man searches reverently for them. God did not make all of His revelations in the past. He is continually revealing Himself, His plans and His truths to those who will search for them."

There are many who feel, they are so evil and wicked. Can they approach God?

God is our mother. If a child falls into a ditch and is covered with filth, what does he do? He runs to his mother and says, "Ma, I have become dirty, cleanse me!"

We must be like that child. We don't have to be afraid to approach our mother.

Religion

There is only one religion, though there are hundred versions of it.
— George Bernard Shaw

All mystics speak the same language,
for they come from the same country.
— Louis- Claude de Saint- Martin

Every prophet and every saint hath a way,
but it leads to God: all the ways are really one.
— Rumi

There are so many who can believe one thing at a time. I am so made as
to rejoice in the many and behold the beauty of the One in the many.
Hence my natural affinity to many religions;
in them all I see revelations of the one spirit. And deep in my heart is the
conviction that I am a servant of all prophets.
— Sadhu Vaswani

Dadaji, if there is only one God, how come there are so many deities in our religion? How do we know which one to believe in?

Why are there so many coloured dresses? Imagine if you all were wearing grey, how would you like it? God is one but that One has many forms. You can go to Him in any form that appeals to you. Everyone of them is His form.

Consider this example. At home, you address your father as daddy. When he goes to the office, he is a boss and not a daddy. When he goes to the club, he is only a friend. But he is still the same. God is one but He has many forms; each man must choose the form which suits his temperament.

You go to a garden. If you had only one type of flower, how would you like that garden? You would not like to visit it again. It is only because you have myriad coloured flowers in a garden that you like to go to the garden. Out of so many types of flowers, you choose one.

India has specialised in spirituality as the West has specialised in technology, in science. In India you have spiritual food which could be given to a primitive or which could be given to a man with the greatest intellect in the world. The primitive man is happy with the stone. He puts red *sindoor* on the stone and treats it as God. The intellectual will not do so. For the intellectual there is another type of food.

Why is there rivalry in religion?

Rivalry in religion is meaningless. There can be no rivalry in true religion. As it seems to me, rivalry is due to two things— want of knowledge and lack of sympathy. Sometimes, there is lack of sympathy. And often, I think, there is lack of both.

There are some who believe that they have the one full and final revelation of the Spirit; so that those, who stand outside the circle of their own faith, must necessarily be in error. Again, there are some who approach the religious problem in no spirit of sympathy. They fix their attention on certain aberrations and extravagancies of a particular religion and say, "Look here, this religion is a monstrosity!"

So it is that quarrels, discord and hatred, have entered the religious world. Religion, which was meant to be a bond of union, has become a source of sectarian strifes.

Why have so many lost faith in religion today?

Men, today, have lost faith in religion, because religion has been separated from life. Religion will come into its own when men will learn to live amicably and helpfully with their fellow-men. Civilisation is sinking, for there is lack of unity in our lives. Civilisation may be saved if life is built in the vision of the One-in-all.

Is it true that one cannot attain to God if one does not belong to a particular religion?

In the Kingdom of God, the Kingdom of Heaven, there are no Hindus or Christians or Muslims. In the Kingdom of God, we will not be judged according to our labels or the creeds we believe in, but according to the life that we have lived. On one occasion, Jesus admonished his disciples and said to them, "Here you call me Lord, but in the Kingdom of Heaven I shall say, I know you not." He also said, you must not be hearers of the Word, but doers of the Word." It is life that is needed, not creeds, not dogmas, not labels or professions.

If a man wears a woman's clothes, he does not become a woman. If a woman wears a man's clothes, she does not become a man. If an ignorant man wears a stethoscope, he does not become a doctor, though he may look like one. What is needed is a heart in which the

ation
geism. Violent
Seeker Service Silence Spiri
Vibrations Willpower Woman
Of The World Bhagavad Gi
Selfishness, Frustration. W
Rituals Sadhu Vaswani Scie
Thought Power Understanding
Education Faith Fear Forg
Meditation M
And

Spirit of God dwells— a heart full of longing and love, longing for the Lord and love for all who suffer and are in pain. Such a heart a person can have, even though he is not a member of any church. If you would help humanity to move on the upward path, convert the minds and hearts of people, do not tell them to change their religions.

Dada, there are so many people who claim that their religion is better than all other religions. Is this right?

Religion is like a mother. And all religions are sisters. If Hinduism is my mother, Christianity is my aunt. I often say, "If Krishna is my father, Christ is my uncle!"

All mothers may not be equal in virtue or intelligence: but it is natural for everyone to regard his own mother as the best in the world. Each one honestly believes that his religion is the best. Among my friends are people belonging to different religions: and we have found that there is a basic unity among all religions. This basic unity, not the differences, must be emphasised, if we are to have peace in the world. If I regard my religion as the best and consider other religions as inferior to mine, there will surely be quarrels and strife among the people of the earth. Behind the desire to convert is the belief that my religion is superior to that of the person whom I seek to convert. This is what leads to discord and strife.

Everyone regards his own mother as the best, but that does not prevent him from learning something from his aunts. Neither on that account would he expect or ask others to give up their mothers and adopt his own.

You do not choose the family in which you are born, nor even the religion to which you belong. The choice is made by God and is for your highest good.

Dada, we stand on the threshold of a new millennium. What is the best way of entering it?

Let us step into the new millennium with the faith that He who has taken care of us so long will not lose hold of us. He is by us, besides us, with us, guarding us, guiding us, leading us on!

All around us, today, is a ring of darkness. But darkness cannot stay forever. When I look into the future, it is so bright, it burns my eyes. It is up to each one of us to make this future a reality.

Let each one of us kindle a little light— a little lamp of kindness and courage and compassion. Let us plant shady trees under which we will not sit. Let us do little acts of kindness. Is not kindness better than knowledge, more important than wisdom?

Let us be a little more kind than necessary. Be kind, for who knows the next person you meet carries a hurt in his heart. Let us do what little we can to help make the world a better place to live in. The greatest mistake is his who does nothing because he can do only a little!

Rituals

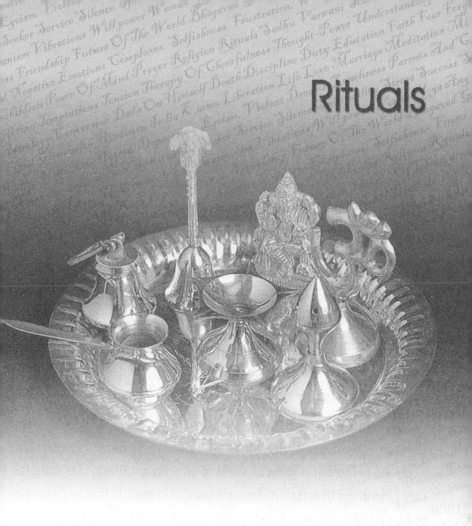

Of all rites the holiest rite
Is to cleanse one's soul in the company of the saints.
— Hymns of Guru Arjan, 16th century

any devout soul offers me with devotion a leaf or flower or fruit or water,
I enjoy that offering of devotion.
— Bhagavad Gita, 9, 26

Why are some of us so involved with rituals?

Why is it that in the season of autumn, all leaves drop out of the trees? You find only the branches. Why? It is part of nature. Religion too passes through seasons. When religion is in its spring season, it is a most wonderful thing.

Every religion when it began, began with a spring season. There were the great ones who formulated religion— just to meet them was to feel elevated. They passed away. Then set in the summer season. There were those that had met and known the great ones and even to come into contact with them was a great blessing. Then religion grew and the autumn season came.

Now I believe we are in the winter season of religion. But every winter, mind you, gives place to spring. The spring is coming. Let us herald that spring season.

The rituals are necessary because in the winter season of every religion, if we did not have rituals, religion would die. It is rituals that keep the name of religion alive. It is only an ancillary, it is only the outer covering of religion. True religion is in the life that we live. Let us be inspired to bear witness to the true ideal which is at the centre of every religion, at the essence of every religion. And that is love. If you build your life according to the law of love, you will never be wrong. You will lack nothing.

What is the deeper significance of prasadi?

The literal meaning of the word *prasad* is grace. *Prasad* is sacred food. It is a sacrament. When you come to a house of worship, a house of God, you are given *prasad* which is only a symbol of blessing. The idea behind *prasad* is that it contains a vibration of blessing. We take that blessing with ourselves. Therefore, there are people who take

Dadaji, is it wrong to pluck flowers and offer them to God?

Sadhu Vaswani believed that we must not pluck flowers. They live in families. They don't want to be separated from each other.

Secondly, when you pluck a flower, it is like killing a flower. The flower dies. Let the flower die a natural death. When it drops down, you can pick it up. But there are people who say there is no harm in offering it to God. So it all depends upon your own belief. You have to make the choice.

Mahatma Gandhi, Sadhu Vaswani and several other great ones were not in favour of plucking flowers. Sadhu Vaswani never wished to accept a flower garland.

Why do people offer animal sacrificers to *Kali Ma* on auspicious days of *Navratri*?

I don't know how this entered into the life of religion. Originally there were no animal sacrifices. We have the word *yagna* in the *vedas*. The literal meaning of the word *yagna*, is sacrifice. But it is the sacrifice of the ego, the sacrifice of the *pancha vikaras*— *kama, krodh, lobh, moha, ahankara*. These *vikaras* have been called animals. So they say again and again, you must sacrifice the five animals within you. Then gradually people began to say, if we are unable to sacrifice the animal within us, let us sacrifice the animals that are outside. May be, that is how the idea of animal sacrifice came up.

Over twenty five centuries ago, Gautama Buddha came and raised his voice against animal sacrifices. He said, you must sacrifice the animal within you. Of what use is it to sacrifice goats and lambs? It gives us no benefit, rather it binds us to more *karma*.

What is the real meaning and purpose of *aarati*?

Every organisation has different rituals and rules. Let these not confound you. These are but outer things. At its core, *aarati* is an invocation of the *Ishtadeva*, the *gurudeva* or God.

When we are doing *aarati* we wave a light with the aspiration that the same light we are waving around, may be kindled within us.

Why don't all Hindus sing the same *aarati*?

Within every religion there are different sects, which perform different rituals. Manifestation means variety and diversity. Yet behind all diversity, there is unity. Remember, all *aaratis* are addressed to the One *shakti*, the One without a second. Glorify that One!

How can bhajans help in increasing spirituality? Isn't it better to meditate?

The idea is to forget the body, to transcend them both, to move away from the body and mind consciousness. It all depends on the individual. If *bhajans* help you, then sing *bhajans*. If meditation helps you, then meditate.

We have seen people offering prayers before a meal. Is this necessary?

It is absolutely necessary. In fact, it is a discipline that we would all do well to follow.

There was a king, who found that many of the ministers and officials in the palace never offered a prayer before eating their food. They just devoured it. One day, he invited the beggars of the town for a meal. When they came and sat at the dining table, they found all those delicacies placed in front of them. They simply could not control themselves. Their mouths began to water. They immediately started eating, just grabbing the food.

The ministers and officials, who were in attendance said, "How is it that they are behaving in this nasty manner?" It was then that the king said to them, "That is what so many of us do. When we sit to eat our meals we do not even offer a prayer." The ministers and officials took the hint and after that they started offering a simple prayer of gratitude to the Lord before eating their food. We too must do likewise, everyday.

Now when we return to our homes we will have dinner. But perhaps when we see the dinner, that warm food in front of us, we will forget what has been said. We will start gobbling it. In the middle of eating if we remember, we should stop eating, fold our hands, close our eyes and offer a prayer of gratitude to the Lord and continue our meal.

Remember, the food that is eaten as *prasadam*, purifies you. "Lord touch this food that has been placed in front of me as *prasadam* and so bless me that every ounce of energy that I get out of it is spent in the service of the poor and broken one, in the service of birds and animals, in the service of all life. Thou art giving me food for the body, grant me sustenance for the soul. And so bless me that I may fulfil the purpose for which thou hast sent me to this earth plane and bless thou every one of those without whom this food would not have reached me. Blessed be Thy Name!"

What is the significance of havan ?

The *havan* is such a beautiful ceremony! It brings blessings on the place where the sacred fire is kindled and it purifies the entire atmosphere. The one good thing about *havan* is when you offer ghee, clarified butter, in the fire it purifies the entire atmosphere. You call it a ritual but in Germany and even in Russia they are carrying on experiments to prove scientifically that the place where the *havan* fire is kindled regularly, becomes a place of healing. The ash that they get out of the *havan* is mixed with the soil, and this, in many cases, has yielded better crops. When you look at the fire— its leaping flames wake up within you certain emotions which, in itself is purifying.

The *havan* also helps you to evolve spiritually. Of course, we are told, in the ancient books that *agni* is a messenger of the gods.

Do different mantras have different effects ?

Mantras are certain vital words that have come into combination. The great American philosopher, Ralph Waldo Emerson said, "Cut a vital word and it will bleed." In combination, words can generate tremendous power and create wonderful ideas. Certain words have the power to make you lose your temper. If they are capable of doing so, why can't words have the power to elevate consciousness to holy heights?

Sadhu Vaswani

*I have great respect for the saintly character and life of
the late Sadhu T.L. Vaswani. His life has been an example of great
simplicity and utter dedication and many people in different parts of this
country and elsewhere are indebted to him for the spiritual enlightenment
they received from his work and writings.*
– Dr. S. Radhakrishnan

*T.L. Vaswani is a saint of the first water … His mind is filled with lovely
thoughts, and he possesses a wonderful gift of expression, so that his
writings are a joy to read.*
– Henry Thomas Hamblin

Who was Sadhu Vaswani?

He was at once a seer and a sage. He was a saint who did not hide himself in an ivory tower, but mingled as a man amongst men. "Mingle! Mingle!" He said to us, again and again, "Don't be single! For, remember, life and all the bounties of life are given to you as a trust to be spent in the service of the poor and broken ones, the forsaken and forlorn, the untouchable and the outcast, brother birds and animals."

He was a poet, a philosopher, a thinker and an educationist. He was a mystic and a humanitarian. He was the voice of the voiceless ones, the dumb, defenceless children of God, who alas! are being slain by the million in our soulless cities everyday. He said, "I have seen God's image shining in birds and animals and for me not to love bird and animal would be not to love the Lord."

He was a patriot of the purest ray serene and for sometime worked as a close associate of Mahatma Gandhi in the non co-operation movement. But after some time, he quietly slipped out of the vanguard of the freedom movement and devoted his time and energies to more constructive work. In those days, in the early twenties, the question was asked of him, "Do you think freedom will come to India?" He said, "Freedom is coming to India, sure as the sun rises in the east, but my one anxiety is this, when freedom comes to India, may India not be found lacking." "Therefore," even in those days he said, "what we need are men and women of character, men and women of sterling qualities, who may take charge of the administration and who may be in charge of different spheres of our activities."

Sadhu Vaswani opened *ashramas*. He started *yuvak sanghas*, youth centres. He founded the Mira Movement which is an experiment in new education.

"New India", he said "will not be built in the Loksabha or the Rajyasabha, but New India will be built in the home and in the school." Therefore give to your children the right type of training in the home, and the right type of education in the school.

What was the essential message of Sadhu Vaswani?

Sadhu Vaswani was a man of tremendous spiritual magnetism. He believed that the noblest work is to cultivate the soul. Every man, he taught, must do his duties sincerely and earnestly, and at the same time spend some time in prayer, meditation, repetition of the Name Divine. He also believed that if a person would be happy, he must make others happy. He taught that children are the richest treasure of a society, a community, and of humanity: Therefore, they should receive proper training at home and right type of education in the school and college. He taught us that to serve the poor and the lowly, the unwanted and the unloved, is truly to worship God. He said repeatedly: "The day I have not served someone in need, is a lost day indeed."

Dada, has the Sadhu Vaswani Mission started a new religious cult?

No, the world does not need new religious cults, but new life. So many rites: so many creeds. What the sad world needs is the life of sympathy and love. Sadhu Vaswani said, again and again, "Religion? Let us talk of it less, practise more!" The emphasis of Sadhu Vaswani was on life, not on words, nor on rites, rituals, creeds," dogmas. "Creeds," he said, "are broken reeds and dogmas divide. But religion, true religion is life. True religion is that which teaches us to love God and to serve the God in man. For within every man there dwelleth God. Every man is a living, moving temple of God. To render service to man is truly to worship God."

Tell us something about Sadhu Vaswani— some significant incident from his life.

I could give you many moving, deeply touching incidents from the pure, gentle, love-filled life of Sadhu Vaswani. One day, as he took a walk on the roadside, he saw someone lying underneath a tree. He was a beggar. His clothes were tattered and torn, his feet were soiled with mud. Sadhu Vaswani asked for a bucket of water. As soon as the bucket was brought, Sadhu Vaswani, this uncrowned king of our hearts— he had but to lift up a finger and hundreds of us would rush to find out what his wish was— with his own hands, he washed the body of the beggar and gave him his own shirt to wear. The beggar pointed to the cap on Sadhu Vaswani's head. Without the least hesitation, Sadhu Vaswani passed on his cap to the beggar.

On that occasion, Sadhu Vaswani spoke words which I can never forget. He said, "This shirt and this cap and everything I have, is a loan given to me to be passed on to those whose need is greater than mine!"

In those words is enshrined a teaching, which if put into practice, can change the face of the world. Everything we have— our time and talent, our knowledge and experience, our wisdom, our money and possessions, our energy and enthusiasm, our influence and authority, our life itself— is a loan given to us to be passed on to those whose need is greater than ours.

This is the ideal placed before the Sadhu Vaswani Mission. I confess we are still far, very far from the ideal. But there is comfort in the thought that there are some, in our midst, who seek to bear witness to it in deeds of daily living.

What was Sadhu Vaswani's message for humanity?

The beloved Master's message can be summed up in what I call the blessed eight-fold path. The steps on the path are:

ction Life...
golism, Violent Dream... Spirituality
eker Service Silence Will power Woman Yoga...
Vibrations Of The World Bhagavad Gita... Frustration, Worry
Selfishness, Rituals Sadhu Vaswani Science...
Thought Power Education Faith Fear Forg
Understanding... Meditation M
And

1.   Man is a pilgrim, a wayfarer. His pilgrimage is to the eternal, where is his true home. Nothing here belongs to him. Everything is given him for use. He must use it wisely and well.

2.   Man has wandered outside himself. He needs to embark on the interior pilgrimage.

3.   He must practise silence everyday and, sinking deeper and deeper within, behold the imprisoned splendour. Sadhu Vaswani's emphasis was more on the unfolding of the heart thus on development of brain power. "Awaken thy heart, O man!" he said, again and again.

4.   To be able to do so he must annihilate the ego, and walk what Sadhu Vaswani called, "the little way".

5.   The non-egoistic man is a picture of forgiveness. He does not remember the hurts that have been inflicted on him.

6.   The non-egoistic man has surrendered his will to the Will Divine. He greets every happening with the *mantra*, "I accept!"

7.   The heart of such a man is filled with divine love. He beholds God face to face.

8.   He feels the thrill of the presence of God in all that is around him. And he becomes a servant of those who suffer and are in pain.

Science and Spirituality

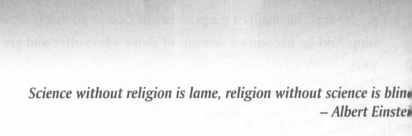

Science without religion is lame, religion without science is blind.
– Albert Einstein

ation Life
gotism Violent Dream
Seeker Service Silence Spirituality Will power Woman Yoga
Of The World Bhagavad Gita
Selfishness Frustration Worry Science
Rituals Sadhu Vaswani Power Understanding
Thought Power Education Faith Fear For
Meditation

Is there a conflict between science and spirituality?

The word for spirituality in Sanskrit is *atma vidya*— *vidya* means science, *atma vidya* is science of the Spirit. Spirituality, too, is a science. It concerns the discovery of the one Self in all.

People are awed by the miracles of science as much as they are fascinated by the powers of spirituality. There is no competition between the two. Spirituality is discovery of the Self. Science is the discovery of nature's laws. In the final analysis, there is no difference; both are discoveries; both are an experience of an "awareness". Our *rishis* had this knowledge. They had gained the knowledge of science through intuition. So there is no difference.

Isn't it a fact that science is misused in today's world?

What you say about science does not apply to pure science. It refers only to applied science. Pure science may be pursued for the sake of science— knowledge for the sake of knowledge.

When science becomes applied, it becomes a source of power which may be both beneficial or destructive, depending on how we use it. That is where the heart comes in. If the heart is pure, kind, compassionate, it will never make wrong decisions. When the scientists learnt to split the atom and release the tremendous power that lies locked up within its nucleus, the very first use they made of the discovery was to rain death and destruction on Hiroshima and Nagasaki. The problem of science lies in its misuse, because man's heart is not awakened. Science, today, has become more of a curse than a blessing.

On the other hand, think of the ancient Chinese. When they invented gunpowder, they never used it for destructive purposes. They used it to make their children happy by manufacturing fire-crackers!

Do you believe that history repeats itself— in the sense that Hiroshima and Nagasaki might happen again, only on a much larger scale?

Yes, if it happens again, it will be on a much larger scale. Let us all pray that such a situation is averted.

They asked George Bernard Shaw what he thought about the Third World War. In his inimitable way, he replied that he couldn't say anything about the Third World War, but if there was a Fourth World War, people would fight with sticks and stones!

There is hope for humanity if we begin with the child. The hope lies in a new type of education.

Can there be a spiritual approach to matters of science?

There is an interaction and a unity between spirituality and science. There is, today, a trend that seeks to work out an integration between science and spirituality. A number of scientists including Nobel Laureates have said that we are busy studying the electron— what if the electron were to turn around and ask, "Who is this entity who is trying to study us?" This takes us to the fundamental question, what is man? What am I? This makes many of us feel that science is now only one step away from spirituality, from *Vedanta*. When scientists are able to answer this question there will be total integration between science and spirituality.

Do you believe that much physical illness has spiritual causes and as such, may be cured through spiritualism?

I prefer the word spirituality to spiritualism. Spiritualism may be understood by some as the art of contacting spirits of the dead ones.

It cannot be denied that the skills of modern medicine are amazing. The miracles of healing performed by modern medicine are astounding. It is dreadful to think what would have been the fate of humanity if medical researchers had not made the astonishing discoveries which they have. And yet I believe that the time has come when modern medicine must take a step forward.

As it is, modern medicine treats only the body— or, at best, the body-mind complex— neglecting the subtler dimensions of the human being. Modern medicine considers the body to be a machine which can be repaired when it goes out of order. The truth is that the body is only a superficial part of what we are. The body is only a jacket which we have worn: we are the wearers of the jacket.

Man is a composite being built up of body, mind and soul. The body, according to the *Gita*, is only a garment we have worn. The mind is an instrument we have brought with ourselves to do our work on the physical plane. Essentially, we are the soul. If the soul be sick, do whatever you will with the body, it will keep on moving from one sickness to another.

When I was a school student, tuberculosis was regarded as an incurable disease. In due course, a cure for T. B. was found. But in the meantime, people started getting hypertension and heart attacks. Angioplasty and open heart surgery were invented. In the meantime, people got cancer— and now it is AIDS. And so it goes on. So long as the soul is sick, the body cannot be truly healthy. We have to treat the whole man.

Seeker

Life is a quest.
— Edna St. Vincent Millai

Pilgrims are we all. Our pilgrimage is to the Eternal where is our Home.
— Sadhu Vaswani

O wanderer! Thy Homeland seeketh thee!
— Sadhu Vaswani

Dada, what should be the ideal of every true seeker?

The ideal of every true seeker of God should be perfection. Each one of us should strive to be perfect. It was Jesus who said, "Be ye perfect even as your Father in Heaven is perfect!" Even as God is perfect, even so must we aspire after perfection. The perfect man, by the Sufis, is called, *kaamil-e-insaan*. Let each one of us strive to be perfect.

Dada, what is the mark of a perfect man?

This, that he wanders not. How much we wander! It may appear that we are seated in one place: but our minds keep on wandering.

"What is the quickest, the fastest thing in the world?" a sage was asked. And he answered, "The mind." See how fast the mind travels— faster than sound, faster than the Concord, faster than light. One moment it is here: another moment it is in New York: a third moment it is in Taiwan. The mind keeps on wandering. It will never be still.

As the mind wanders, we keep on wandering with it. Our bodies may be in one place, but our thoughts are scattered. They keep moving from one place to another, one object to another, one form to another.

Suppose I were to ask you to keep your minds fixed on one object, one idea, just for one single minute, how many of you would be able to do that? Can you keep your minds still just for half a minute? (Half a minute's silence) Tell me, if during that brief, very brief period, was the mind of anyone of you still? If you are sincere, you will tell me that, even in the brief space of half a minute, your minds kept on wandering.

The perfect man is one whose wandering has ceased.

Dada, why does the mind wander?

The cause of wandering is three-fold. *Maya* has three faces, three prongs:

1. The first is pleasure, sense gratification. See how pleasure draws us. The cinema, the theatre, the club, the disco, the snack bar— all these and so many other things fascinate us, wake up desires within us. It is desires that make us wander.

The whole world is running after, is dancing to the tune of desires. This dance of desires is the dance of death. If you would be perfect, keep away from desires. Control your desires: do not let desires control you!

2. The second face, the second prong of *maya* is wealth. We keep on amassing more and more wealth. We do not have the time to spend it! Suddenly, death pounces upon us and, leaving our millions behind, we move on, empty-handed, to the Other Shore.

3. The third face of *maya* is name, fame, earthly greatness, power and authority. There are people who shun pleasures, who keep away from wealth, but who want name and fame, popularity and publicity. They want the applause of the people. They, too, are prisoners of *maya* and do not attain to perfection.

Service

We ourselves feel that what we are doing is just a drop in the ocean. But the ocean would be less because of that missing drop.
– *Mother Teresa*

Did you meet him on the road? Did you leave him with the load?
– Sadhu Vaswani

The earth is my country and to do good is my religion.
– The Vedas

He who cooks for himself alone is a thief. If your house has no bread for a guest or a poor starving man, are you better than a robber on the high road?
– Sadhu Vaswani

Everyone talks of service these days. Can you tell us what true service is?

Service is doing the Will of God. There is nothing beyond it. The world has many doers. But in this critical period of social disorder and chaotic decay, the tortured soul of humanity cries out for Will-doers— those who do the Will of God. So many of our politicians have been doing, doing, doing: they have been doing mischief. So many our social workers have been doing, doing, doing, they have been doing disorder. Their doing has been the undoing of God's plan. We must strive to be Will-doers. Then will our action, blended with *bhakti* (devotion), be radiant with knowledge.

Could you elaborate on Will-doers, please?

We work so strenuously, so hard, and yet achieve nothing. We work for the good of the community, society, nation, humanity. We sacrifice our health, wealth, rest and leisure. Yet our work produces no effect. The world speeds on from danger to destruction. The reason is that our work is not in tune with the divine Will. Our work is tainted with the self— selfish motives, desire for prominence, thoughts of reward in this life or in the life beyond. We have not renounced the ego: we have not offered our lives in the great *yagna* (sacrifice) of the universe.

The man who offers his life, his all, at the Lotus Feet of the Lord, works with peace in his heart. He works as a servant of God and man. He sees that men and women suffer in this world of tragedy and tears. He gives to all the service of love. His work does not take him away from God. His work is God-inspired, God-guided. "Not I, but the Father in me works," he says. His work is ever the work of God. In his work there is no hustle, no bustle, no fuss, no noise, no aimless rushing about. In his work there is no unrest but peace— the peace that passeth understanding. In his work is love for all!

Sometimes, when we do good to others, we are not appreciated. How then will we have the incentive to continue?

Go to the *Gita*— which tells you that you must do good to others without seeking, without having any thought of reward in return, not even a simple word of thanks. That is the way in which good should be done to others. We do good to others, not because of others, but because of God, who resides in others. Within every human being there is God. In the *Gita*, the Lord says, "I am seated in the hearts of all."

When I do good to others, I make of it an offering to Sri Krishna, so I expect nothing in return, rather I am anxious that this good that I want to do is going to be accepted. When we work in this spirit, we work for our own happiness, we work for our own interior peace of mind. So keep on doing as much good as you can, to as many as you can, in as many ways as you can, on as many occasions as you can, and as long as you can— but without expecting anything in return.

"Arjuna, to work you have the right but not to the fruit thereof, not to the reward thereof."

Sadhu Vaswani used to tell us again and again, "The reward of service is more service." That is the only reward we can expect for service— to be given greater opportunities to be of service to others.

Dada, how can we serve in the right way?

To serve aright, you must bear in mind the following five rules. I love to call them the five fingers of service:

1. Serve silently. We have for a long time confounded work with noise. We do a little work and we create much noise. We spend our strength in tumults and shouts. True strength is in silent work.

2. Serve humbly. When you serve, do not think that you are doing *meherbani* to those whom you serve. It should be the other way. When you serve, feel grateful to those who give you a chance to be of service to them. For service is a debt each one has to pay.

3. Serve lovingly. Pour love into your service! How often do we become harsh with those whom we seek to serve! Therefore, identify yourselves with those whom you serve. They are not apart from you; they are a part of you.

4. If you would reform the world, begin with yourself! Let each one mend his own life! Do not interfere with others. Service is not interference. A true server realises that he must mend his own life.

5. The fifth finger of service is, "If you would serve aright, cultivate the soul!" Cultivate the soul! Therefore, know that you are only a tool, an instrument. God is the One Worker. Cultivate the soul! Therefore, do not confound the means with the end. Renouncing all egoism and selfishness, become instruments of the eternal *shakti* that shapes the lives of individuals and nations.

Silence

Silence is the speech of the spiritual seeker.
— Sathya Sai Baba

There is silence which frightens. It is the silence of vacant space.
But the silence filled with the presence of God and His Angels is uplifting.
It is the Silence that speaks.
— Sadhu Vaswani

What is silence ?

Silence, is two-fold. There is the outer silence: it is absence of noise, freedom from the shouts and tumults of daily life. And there is interior silence: it is freedom from the clamour of desires, cessation of mental acrobatics, stilling of the play of conflicting forces. It is the peace that passeth, that surpasseth understanding. The seers of ancient India called it *"turiya"*, which means the "fourth". It is the fourth stage. May you and I aspire to reach this stage! Not until we have reached it, may we hope to experience unbroken joy and peace and harmony for which our distracted hearts have been crying.

You often speak of silence as an appointment with God. How can we cultivate this silence in this age of technology, where we are surrounded by sounds and activity?

It is a fact that the great need of modern man is silence. To help us to avoid stress and tension, the noted psychologist, Deborah Bright, recommends twenty minutes of PQT twice a day. PQT stands for personal quiet time.

Even as particles of dust cling to our clothes, so too, particles of noise cling to our hearts. To clean our clothes, we wash them with soap and water. Even so, to cleanse our souls, we need to take a dip in the waters of silence. Thus, it is necessary to practise silence every day.

Can silence heal?

We live in a world of allurements and entanglements. The sharp arrows of desire, craving, animal appetite, of passion and pride, of ignorance, of hatred and greed, wound our souls again and again. Our souls bear the scars of many wounds. They need to be healed. Silence is the great healer.

Why is silence said to be golden? Is not speech a great gift given to us?

Let silence be the law of your life: for silence hurts no one. When you feel like breaking your silence, ask yourself if what you have to say is something better than silence. If so, say it; else remain silent.

If only we could collect the words each one of us speaks, what a huge mountain they would make! Himalayas of words have passed through these tiny lips. All these words come under five categories:

1. Words inspired by love of God. These are the words we utter in adoration of the Eternal— the cry of the soul to the Over Soul, the songs sung in praise of the Most High, prayer, *kirtan* and *japa* of the sacred Name.

2. Words inspired by love of fellow-men. These are the words of comfort and consolation we pass on to those who suffer and struggle and are in sorrow— words which cheer them on life's lonesome way.

3. Words which wound and hurt and kill. These are the words inspired by jealousy, envy, anger, malice or hatred. How often do we not speak ill of others, little knowing what havoc we cause! An archer shoots to kill. More dangerous is the man with a forked tongue. Every time he opens his lips, he sends forth shafts which strike and sting.

4. Words inspired by self-love. These are the words prompted by egoism, by greed and sensuality. How often do we not brag about our so-called achievements or speak in self-righteous pride! And see, how happy men feel when they indulge in obscene and sensual talk! When it comes to making

an untruth. They gain a little and lose their all.

5. Idle words. These are the words men utter without rhyme or reason, merely to while away their time. The conversations of men are filled with silly questions and imbecile answers, which make our homes centres of idle gossip and our clubs and meeting-places so many 'Towers of Babel'. Against this type of talk did Jesus warn, when he said, "But I say unto you, that for every idle word that men speak, they shall have to render account, on the day of judgement." This saying is not given us in the Gospels, but in one of the Eastern accounts of Jesus.

When you purchase an earthen-vessel, you strike it, and from the sound, make out if it is cracked or not. So, too, is the integrity of man proved by his speech. If the words a man utters belong to the first two classes, verily is he blessed among mortals. Such a one spreads sunshine wherever he goes!

Is it true that silence can give us insight into our lives— tell us where we come from, what we are doing and where we will go from here ?

As you enter into silence, you will realise this truth— that you are from the Kingdom of God, that you are going to the Kingdom of God, and that this Kingdom of God is not apart from you, it is right within you!

Our journey is an interior journey. It is the journey in consciousness. Today, we find that for many of us, our consciousness is imprisoned in what we call the lower *chakras*. Silence can be a process by which we may free our consciousness from such low feelings, and raising it step by step, we may arrive at the Kingdom of God within us. We don't have to ascend the skies to reach heaven. It is right here, within us.

All spiritual teachers tell us that we are dwellers in the dark.
What is the way of coming out of the darkness that envelops us?

It is the way of turning within! Alas, we are busy with many things, but have neglected the one thing needful. We keep chasing shadow-shapes which come and go. When shall we learn to turn within?

Man came to the earth as a pilgrim, but has become a wanderer. Even in our spiritual quest, we wander from creed to creed, from one school of thought to another, and are filled with unrest. We move to temples and churches and places of pilgrimage, and meet with disappointment. For, not until we turn within, will we find that which we are seeking.

Truth is within! Wisdom is within! The source of all strength is within! Therefore, turn within!

A beginning has to be made somewhere. Every day, preferably at the same time and at the same place, let us sit in silence and pray, meditate, do our spiritual thinking. It is our daily appointment with God. We keep a number of appointments, every day. Alas! we neglect this most important of all appointments— our daily appointment with God. He is not far away from us. He is wherever we are. He is here: He is now! All we have to do is to close our eyes, shut out the world and call Him— and there He is in front of us. In the beginning we may not see Him: but let us be sure, that He sees us. We may not be able to immediately hear His voice: but He hears us. The tiniest whisper of the human heart, the smallest stirring of the soul is audible to His ever-attentive ears. Speak to Him: open out your heart to Him: place all your difficulties before Him: and you will find wonderful things happen to you.

Spirituality

To know others is wisdom, to know oneself enlightenment.
– Tao Te Ching

I have read many spiritual books but I get confused. What should I do?

Don't read many books. Too much reading confuses. It is like going to a new place and studying guide books. They will take you nowhere. You must have a guide to take you to a place. Likewise, in spiritual life you must have a guide— who for want of a better word we call the Guru— who can take you to the Goal. For that it is necessary to have longing of the heart. Pray to the Lord to put you in touch with such a one.

What is Vedanta? Can you explain it to us in simple terms?

Vedanta is the culmination of all Vedic knowledge. This knowledge can be summed up briefly in these words; there is the One in all. The vision of the One-in-all is *Vedanta*. When I behold the One-in-all, the One whom for want of a better word we call God, that is true *Vedanta*. When I see God not only in the good, but in those whom the world calls bad, evil, then I have attained to true knowledge.

Of Swami Vivekananda, it was asked, "Tell us what is *Vedanta*, in a few simple words." He replied, "In a few simple words, *Vedanta* is the knowledge that I and my brother are one." My brother– the beggar, the cripple, the blind man and the criminal— and I are one. That is *Vedanta*— beholding the One in all.

Is aspiring for normal material happiness an impediment on the path of spirituality?

If you move on the path of spirituality, then you do not aspire for anything material. You leave it to the Lord.

"God, I want to make of my life an offering at your Lotus

Feet," this is the aspiration of a true seeker's heart. Then it is for God to give you whatever He likes. God is our Master and He is a very benevolent Master. If only you surrender your life at His Lotus Feet, you will find miracles happening in your daily life.

"Seek ye first the Kingdom of Heaven and all these things shall be added unto you," said Jesus.

Spiritual aspirants are forced to lead a dual life. There is a conflict between spirituality and the world. What should an aspirant do?

The great teacher of humanity, Jesus, said on one occasion, "You cannot serve two masters at the same time." At every step, life presents us with choices. We have to make the decision. If you have two masters, a time will come when one master will ask you to move in one direction, the other will ask you to move in the opposite direction. So you have to make a choice— the Word or the world.

The spiritual path is essentially a path of sacrifice. Before a person steps on the spiritual path, he realises the vanity of all that is around him. Such a person is prepared to sacrifice anything.

A little boy came regularly to the *satsang*. One day, I asked him, "What is it that you want— God or money?

He thought for a while and said, "Give me some time, I will come back to you!"

The next day he met me and said, "I could not sleep last night. I thought and pondered over what you asked me. To tell you the truth— I want both— God and the world!" You cannot lift two melons in one hand. You have to make a choice!

Is it possible for a person not to leave his house and his business and still continue to be on the spiritual path?

You don't have to leave your home, your business. All you have to leave is your sense of I-ness and mine-ness.

How can we find the absolute truth?

Most of us are happy with what our conscience tells us to do. That is, we are happy with our own social restraints. There are very few who feel inspired to set out in quest of the absolute. You have such people in every country, race and religion. They go beyond the social restraints. This takes immense effort and it needs the grace of God. "Thousands set out in quest, but very few find." They that are chosen, find the Absolute.

How can we wash off all the impurities that cling to our souls?

Service to a *satpurkha* is, perhaps, the simplest, easiest way by which we may wash off our impurities. The impurities are many. And until they go, the Light will not shine. We shall continue to dwell in the darkness of ignorance, *avidya*. For *vidya*, true knowledge, is not a matter of words. *Gyana*, wisdom is not book knowledge. I may have memorised a hundred scriptures by heart, I may have delivered a thousand learned discourses on spiritual topics, I am still far from *gyana*, if the Light hasn't awakened within me. For *gyana* is illumination.

What is *tapasya*?

Tapasya is of two kinds, *yama* and *niyama*. Yama is control of the mind. *Niyama* is control of the senses. Everyone of the senses must be controlled.

An ancient Chinese proverb says, "He who conquers a city is great: he who conquers himself is mighty." And for self-conquest, the mind must be kept in harness and every one of the senses must be held in check.

If it is true that we were born into this world for a higher purpose, how is it that so many people are leading a life of sense-gratification, while only few tread the spiritual path?

It is true that many of us have failed to learn the lesson that this life has not been given to us for sense-gratification. The age we live in is *kaliyuga*– and the predominant mark of this age is that people will run after power, pleasure and sense-gratification. The lives of most of us in this age, will be centered on our lower natures.

But this should not discourage you from joining that small minority who realise that life is meant for a higher purpose. Man is not an animal; he can rise to the status of a God, if he tries; he can even become Godlike. This is the great opportunity given to us, as human beings.

People have chosen different paths in their lives. Some of them are engrossed in worldly affairs, while others are immersed in spiritual life. Why is this so? Doesn't the Lord want all of us to reach Him?

This is like asking the principal of a school, "Why are there different classes in your school? Why is it that some children are in the first standard, while some are in the eleventh standard? Don't you want all your students to pass the highest examination?" Yes, the principal would like all his students to pass the highest examination, eventually. But in order to do that, they have to go through different stages of education. Likewise, the Lord wants each and every one of us to reach Him. But we have to pass through different stages to attain to Him. We are all at different

How can I become a better person?

By being a better person surely! The first thing you must do is to realise the flaws in your nature. Every one of us has some weaknesses, some, imperfections. Try to assess your own weaknesses, and then select just one to work on. If you try to tackle all your flaws at once you may not succeed. Select just one weakness and tell yourself, "By the grace of God, I shall overcome this weakness in me." Keep your attention focused on this effort. Don't dwell on the weakness itself— it will only strengthen the weakness. Focus on your resolution to conquer it.

For instance, if there is a man easily given to anger, he must not think of his temper, but of its opposite quality— serenity, peace and tranquillity. The more you focus on this quality, the sooner you will find that this quality enters your being. Remember you become what you think— this is the great law of life. Think better thoughts, higher thoughts, and you will surely become a better person!

Stress

Only the man who can relax is able to create, and ideas reach his mind like lightening.
– Cicero

In the name of God, stop a moment, cease your work, look around you.
– Leo Tolstoy

What is the secret of relaxation?

The secret of relaxation is in the three words, "Let it go!" Life is full of incidents, both pleasant and unpleasant. When an unpleasant thing happens, we are apt to lose our balance; this creates a negative emotion which expresses itself in a feeling of sadness or depression. An effective way of dealing with such a situation is to go to the root of the matter and "let go" what is causing the negative emotion. Let it go! Let everything go!

Has my sister failed to understand me? Let it go! Has my brother spoken ill of me? Let it go! Has my best friend turned against me? Let it go! Have I suffered loss in business? Let it go! Have my plans been upset? Let it go! Have I been treated with disrespect? Let it go! Has a dear one passed on? Let it go! Has my health suffered a setback? Let it go! Have I been cheated, robbed, deceived by someone in whom I have placed my trust? Let it go! In this world of transitoriness, a world in which things come and go and nothing abides, is there anything worth worrying over? Let it go! The more we let go, the more do we conserve our energies for the constructive and creative tasks of life.

Dada, how can we overcome stress?

To overcome stress, you need to understand what stress stands for.

1. S—smile. Keep smiling.
2. T—tolerance. Grow in tolerance.
3. R—relax. Never be tensed.
4. E—easy. Take it easy but be not lazy.
5. S—service. Keep serving.
6. S—silence. Practise silence and thereby turn to God.

People are caught up in the strain and stress of modern life. Do you have an easy formula to draw them to the best of values which you have initiated again and again, in your talks and lectures?

The formula is a three-fold one. Firstly, we must be careful to see that we always have a positive attitude towards life. By positive attitude, I do not mean that life does not have a negative side. Life does have a negative, a dark side. Life is full of difficulties and dangers, trials and tribulations. But the man with the positive approach refuses to dwell on the negative side of life. Surrounded by the most adverse conditions, he will look for a place to stand on. Conditions all around him may be frustrating, but he will not give up. He will continue to expect the best results and this is an inviolable law of life. What you expect persistently, comes rushing to you. For you only draw to yourselves, that which you think of all the time. Your thoughts are magnets. Through our thoughts, we draw to ourselves conditions and circumstances of which we keep on thinking all the time.

Always have a constructive, positive approach towards life. There is a picture I saw many years ago. It is a picture of two buckets, each half filled with water. Outside one bucket, there was a face with a frown and underneath were written the words, "Of what use is it to be half empty all the time?" Outside the other bucket, there was a face with a smile and underneath were the words, "I feel grateful to God that I am at least half full all the time." The two buckets symbolise the negative and positive attitudes towards life. The man with the negative attitude wears a frown on his face. He is always resentful and morose. He feels rejected, unwanted and is never happy. He cannot face the stress and strain of life in the right spirit. The man with the positive attitude wears a smile on his face, is buoyant, full of energy. He has the strength to face the difficulties and dangers of life, in the right spirit.

The second point of the formula is, we must not offer resistance to life. Life has given me many things. Some of them are good. Some of them are not as good. I must accept them all and make the most of them. Of course, I must not be fatalistic. I must not take this lying down. But if, in spite of my best efforts, I am not able to achieve the desired results, I must accept the situation. Acceptance is not a passive thing. To accept is to triumph over circumstances and not let them touch the joy and the peace of the soul. Resistance inevitably leads to wastage of energy which could be used to constructive ends. Do your very best to achieve your desired results, but, if in spite of your efforts, if you fail, let that not depress you. The great Cosmic Power that controls the universe knows what is good for you. So accept, and rejoice!

The third point in the formula is that we must always see the good in others. As the Baha'i prophet, Baha'u'llah, said: If a brother has nine virtues and one fault, let us think of his nine qualities and forget the one fault. If a brother has nine faults and one virtue, let us consider his one virtue and forget the nine faults. That which we see in others has a knack of shifting into us. If we consider the faults of others, they will, in due course, become part of our own nature.

Success

To laugh often and much, to win the respect of intelligent people and the affection of children; to leave the world a bit better, to know even one life had breathed easier because you had lived; that is to have succeeded.
— Ralph Waldo Emerson

I couldn't wait for success so I went ahead without it.
— Jonathan Winters

How can success be measured?

Success must not be measured in terms of money, power, prestige, influence, education or standing in society. For a man may have all of these and yet his life may be full of misery, unhappiness, moral corruption and ineffectiveness. Success should be measured by the yardstick of happiness, the ability to be happy and make others happy, the ability to be loved and to love, the ability to remain in peaceful harmony with those around you, with your own self and with God's cosmic laws.

Success has three dimensions— the first is length, which is concerned with a man's material needs, his hopes and aspirations, his desires and dreams. The second dimension is breadth, for the truly successful man should go beyond himself and reach outward to others. The third dimension is height; he must go high and tap the hidden source of supply and wisdom which we call God.

Can you give us a software for success?

The software for success may be spelt out as:

1. Do only that which you feel is right and true. Nothing in life brings about failure more surely than lack of integrity.

2. Do your best each day. Let this be the motto of your life: only the best is good enough for me! When you give to the world the best you have, the best will come back to you.

3. Fully trust in the divine wisdom that designs and orders the scheme of things. There is a meaning of mercy in all that happens.

4. Plan for today. Budget your time. The truly successful man fits 26 hours into a day of 24, cutting down waste. Take care of every moment of your time.

5. Begin the day right! Wake up, each morning, full of hope and expectation.

6. Never give up! Persistence is the law of success!

7. Tact is better than talent.

8. Stay young all your life! Age is a state of mind.

9. Reach out to others. You succeed in the measure in which you help others to succeed.

Dear Dada, what is a truly successful and fulfilled life?

Success is very often confounded with making money—plenty of money, and with gaining prestige and reputation. True success does not lie in these things. True success is freedom and fulfilment. If you have freedom, if you have fulfilment, you have truly succeeded.

Freedom from what? Freedom from the thralldom of the sense and the mind. We are prisoners.

I remember, several years ago, we were in Karachi and Sadhu Vaswani was taking a walk on the terrace of his house. As he looked down into the street, he exclaimed, "Prisoners! Prisoners!" I looked down, but found no prisoners at all. It was true the house in which we lived was not very far from the Karachi Jail. But there were no prisoners at that time in the street. Some people were walking, some were on bicycles, others were moving about in cars. So I asked Sadhu Vaswani, "Where are the prisoners?" And he said, "Prisoners of desires are the people. Alas, they know not of their bondage!" Yes, we are all prisoners. We are prisoners of desire. But we know not of our bondage. We regard ourselves as free, but we are not. It is when you gain freedom and fulfilment, that you achieve true success.

True success belongs to the person who completely dedicates himself to the Lord, who works on this earth plane only as an instrument of the Lord. In the *Gita*, Sri Krishna says to Arjuna, "You must be a *nimitkarana*. You must go and work as an instrument. Then, when you kill you do not kill." Let us become instruments of the Lord, instruments of His mercy in this world of suffering and pain.

Suffering

All sunshine makes a desert
– Arabic Proverb

I say, next to God, there is no nobler thing than suffering
– Meister Eckhar

What is the best way to handle difficult situations?

Our journey through life has been perfectly planned by Infinite Love and Infinite Wisdom: there can be no mistake. Every experience that comes to us is just the right experience occurring at the right time to train us in the right way. So let us accept all that comes and never attempt to circumvent anything.

Again and again, we try to run away from what appears to us as an unpleasant experience, and try to avoid what we regard as difficult situations. We may succeed in keeping them away for a while, but we can never avoid them all the time, for they are, indeed, essential to our growth. God means us to face them and so to develop our moral and spiritual muscles. If we avoid an unpleasant experience, it will return to us in due course with redoubled force, and we shall be compelled to take up the challenge until we have learnt the lesson it has come to teach us. The best way, therefore, to face difficult situations is to accept them and cooperate with their inner purpose, all the while fixing our mind and heart on Him who has planned for each one of us the glorious liberty that belongs to the children of the Spirit.

What is the cause of our suffering? Taking the question one step further, what is the purpose of all the suffering we go through?

Suffering is of two types. There is the suffering we create for ourselves through violation of the laws of life, through impure thinking and wrong feeling, uncontrolled imagination and unbalanced emotion. Such suffering serves no useful purpose. It can be avoided by bringing our thought, will and imagination under control and by directing our energies to the fulfilment of life's true purpose.

So many of us create unnecessary suffering for ourselves. We cry over spilt milk! We worry over things which have already happened and for which nothing can be done. We let this worry spoil our present; we look with fear to an unknown future.

The future is not in our hands. We may not have a future at all. Or, when it actually comes, it may be so different from what we imagined it to be. The future has been concealed from us by a loving Providence. Why probe into what God chooses to hide from us? To do so is to invite suffering. Bitter is the fruit of man's knowledge. Let us trust without seeing and live without trying to unveil that which has been veiled from our sight. Let us build our life in the words of Jesus which are charged with great practical significance, "Sufficient unto the day is the evil thereof!"

The second type of suffering is that which comes to us from God. It is not due to violation of the laws of life. It comes to the best of men, to the noblest of souls. It came to Krishna and Christ, to Buddha and Zoroaster, to Moses and Muhammad, to Nanak and Kabir, to Chaitanya and Mira, to all lovers of God and Man. This type of suffering does not come alone. It brings with itself the strength which endures, the comfort which lends sweetness to suffering. This is what distinguishes it from the suffering of the first type.

Unaccompanied as it is, by the soothing touch of God, the suffering which man creates for himself becomes hard and unbearable. It breaks down his spirit and throws him into an abyss of gloom.

The suffering which comes to us from God is for our good. We do not understand this until we have cast all thought of self aside. When the self is forgotten, we behold the loving hand of God in every condition and circumstance of life.

Everything that happens, works for our good. The seeming cruelty and injustice of men, their selfishness and ruthless disregard of values we hold dear, are seen to be the result of God's infinite goodness and unfailing love.

How may we know whether we are suffering for the sake of God or for our own wrong doings?

When we suffer for our own sake, even a little of it becomes hard to bear. When we suffer for the sake of God, He takes up the burden and we find the yoke easy to bear.

Significant are the words of Meister Eckhart, the great German mystic, "Believe me, if there was a man willing to suffer on account of God and of God alone, then though he fell a sudden prey to the collective sufferings of all the world, it would not trouble nor bow him down, for God would be the bearer of his burden."

Tell us the best way to tackle suffering.

If our attention is on sufferings, they get magnified beyond all proportions. In the midst of suffering, let us count our blessings. Usually, we suffer only in one area of our life. There are so many other things for which we should be grateful.

Take a piece of paper and make a list of all the blessings you still have. There was a man who started from scratch and built a flourishing business. However, a day came when he became bankrupt. The first thing he did was to take up a piece of paper and write down all the things he still possessed. He found that he still had a great deal to be thankful for. With gratitude in his heart, he started anew and built up a still larger business. If we count our blessings, our suffering recedes into the background.

What gives the saints their healing power? What makes the men of God redeemers of their race?

This, that they receive the arrows of pain as gifts from the All-giver! Alike in sunshine and in rain, they rejoice, give gratitude to God and sing His holy Name. Every great one of humanity has had to bear his cross. Krishna and Buddha and Jesus walked through the valley of the shadow of death. Who are we to say, "We must escape sorrow, anguish, pain?" We, too, must bear our cross, bear and bleed.

And when we bleed, let us remember that the Will of God is working through us: and through suffering and pain, God's Will is purifying us, preparing us for the vision of the one Lord of Life and Light and Love in all that is around us, above us, below us, within us.

Can positive thinking overcome physical pain?

If we want to be unaware of the pain which the body feels, we have to dissociate ourselves from our bodies. The greatest tragedy of man, his greatest illusion, is his identification with the body. I am not this body. This body is only a garment I have worn in this present earth incarnation. I have put on and put off many such bodies through this endless adventure of existence, through which I have passed.

In the measure in which you are able to dissociate yourself from the body, in that measure you will find that pain of the body, will affect you to a lesser degree.

Epictetus was a wise man, one whom I would call a *brahma gyani*. One day, he had a nasty fall and his leg was broken. His friends gathered around him and said to him, "Epictetus, we are so sad to hear that your bone is broken." He laughed and replied, "My bone? I have no bones. It is only the bone of the leg of my body that is broken."

Just imagine such a dissociation! If only we could achieve this, we will not feel physical pain.

Dear Dada, this world is a gift from God and life is supposed to be a learning process. Why do we suffer so much? Can't we learn without all this suffering?

I think we suffer so much because we have not yet realised our true identity. We have to transcend both the body and mind, then there is no suffering at all. It is the mind that creates suffering. If only you transcend the mind there is no suffering at all. But to learn this lesson of transcendence, each one of us has ultimately to transcend the senses. To learn this lesson we have to pass through many painful experiences. And without pain we cannot gain anything. This mind can convert pain into joy, into a source of happiness.

Why is it that bad things happen to good people, while so many who are evil, have the best of life?

Bad things happen to good people that they may grow better, nobler, purer. Even as gold is burnt in the crucible to be cleansed of its dross, even so good people are chosen to burn in the fire of suffering, and so become pure as thrice-burnished gold.

Wealth and pleasures and power and honour are not as good as they seem to be. In many cases, they degrade man and make him corrupt. In our ancient books there is the suggestive story of Kunti. She had to ask for a boon of Lord Krishna. What she asked for was that she might have some little suffering all the time. In suffering, she said, the Lord is remembered; in pleasures and enjoyment, He is forgotten.

How true it is that suffering purifies! Not many know the value of suffering. It was an Indian saint who prayed, "Lord, grant me starvation and sickness and suffering and ignominy!" Those are the things that are of real value to those that know.

Dada, tell us how to face suffering.

In all conditions of life, thank the Lord. Let us make it a habit—to praise the Lord at every step, in every round of life. Even in the midst of fear and frustration, worry and anxiety, depression and disappointment, let these words come out of the very depths of our hearts, "Thank you, God! Thank you, God! Thank you, God!" And we will be filled with a peace that will amaze us. When we thank the Lord all the time, we build for ourselves a ladder of consciousness on which we can climb and touch the very pinnacle of peace.

Let me tell you the story of a woman. Her husband fell seriously ill. The doctors despaired of his condition and said he would not be able to last longer than six months. The woman had deep faith in God and started thanking the Lord a thousand times everyday. "Thank you, God! Thank you, God!" She prayed again and again. "Thank you, God, for having healed my husband and made him whole." She continued to offer this prayer till a few months later, when the husband went for a check up, the doctors were amazed at his miraculous recovery. "A Power above and beyond ours, has been at work!" they exclaimed.

Whatever be the condition in which you find yourself, whatever be the suffering through which you pass, keep on thanking the Lord all the time. When you do so, your heart

ration Violent Silence Spirit
Egoism Violent Silence Spirit
Seeker Service Silence Spirit Woman
Vibrations Willpower Woman
Of The World Bhagavad Gita
Selfishness Frustration Thought Power Understanding
Rituals Sadhu Vaswani Sai
Education Faith Fear For
Meditation M
And

expands and you become receptive to the helpful and healing forces of God.

What is the best way to handle difficult situations?

Our journey through life has been perfectly planned by Infinite Love and Infinite Wisdom: there can be no mistake. Every experience that comes to us is just the right experience occurring at the right time to train us in the right way. So let us accept all that comes and never attempt to circumvent anything.

Again and again, we try to run away from what appears to us as an unpleasant experience, and try to avoid what we regard as difficult situations. We may succeed in keeping them away for a while, but we can never avoid them all the time, for they are, indeed, essential to our growth. God means us to face them and so to develop our moral and spiritual muscles. If we avoid an unpleasant experience, it will return to us in due course with redoubled force, and we shall be compelled to take up the challenge until we have learnt the lesson it has come to teach us. The best way, therefore, to face difficult situations is to accept them and cooperate with their inner purpose, all the while fixing our mind and heart on Him who has planned for each one of us the glorious liberty that belongs to the children of the Spirit.

Temptations

Temptations are the dumb-bells of the soul.
— J.P.V.

What is temptation?

The word temptation is derived from the Latin word tentare, which means to prove, to test. Temptation is the touchstone of the soul. Even as gold is tested on the touchstone, even so man's character, the loftiness of his soul, is tested by the temptations he is able to overcome.

What is the purpose of temptation?

In my boyhood days, I joined a gymnasium. Every morning, I would go and practise my exercise with the dumb-bells. One evening, I asked the instructor, "What is the use of doing this exercise day after day?" He answered, "As you exercise with the dumb-bells, your muscles will be strengthened."

I say to you in answer to your question— temptations are the dumb-bells of the soul. Even as dumb-bells strengthen our physical muscles, even so do temptations strengthen the muscles of the soul. They develop our hidden spiritual strength. Temptations unlock the hidden powers of the Spirit.

Why do we succumb so easily to temptations?

Have you ever looked at a fly sipping honey? At first, it is very careful to see that its legs are free. It sits on the edge of the spoon containing honey, saying to itself that after just one wee little taste of honey, it would fly away. But once it gets the relish of honey, it forgets everything and goes all out for it. When it has had its fill, it finds that its legs are stuck in honey. It cannot fly away and it dies a tragic death in its sweet grave.

Such is the case with man. He is lured into temptation by the thought of a little pleasure that he expects to get. Once he has tasted pleasure, it draws him to itself, again and again, until he becomes the slave of a habit he cannot overcome. Pleasure leads a man astray.

Why does a man commit sin against his will?

Significant are the words of the great law giver, Manu, "Desire is never satisfied by the enjoyment of the objects of desire. It grows from more to more, as does the fire to which fuel is added." And the *Yoga Vasishta* tells us, "We think it is we who enjoy pleasure. But, in truth, it is pleasures that enjoy us. For while pleasure always remains young and vital, it is we who keep growing old and get consumed in the fire of pleasure."

Kama cannot be quenched. The more you seek to satisfy it, the more you add fuel to its flame. *Kama*, desire, lust, reigns over man's unregenerate senses. His reason is clouded: he cannot discriminate between right and wrong: and there are no depths of degradation to which a man, under the influence of *kama*, will not stoop.

Can you give us some practical suggestions to overcome temptation?

1. Temptations are of various types. There is the temptation to gratify the senses; to steal what belongs to another; to drink, to smoke, to take drugs; to overeat or to eat forbidden food or food of violence; to send out thoughts of ill-will to others; to speak harsh words or to indulge in untruth; to gossip, to spread scandals against others; to waste time in playing cards or other frivolities; to accept bribes, to indulge in unlawful profiteering, to make money by means fair or foul; to evade the payment of taxes. There are a hundred and one other temptations. To be able to overcome any type of temptation, you must be ready and willing to turn a new leaf. You must

ration Violence Silence Spu
Egoism Service Silence Spir
Seeker Service Willpower Woman
Vibrations Willpower Woman Be
Of The World Bhagavad G.
Selfishness, Frustration, F
Rituals Sadhu Vaswani Ser
Thought Power Understand
Education Faith Fear For
Meditation M
And C

decide once and for all that you will never, never, fall into sin again.

2. "God, be merciful to me, a sinner!" is a very noble aspiration: but it must not be overdone. We must not indulge in a lot of retrospection. With a heart contrite and lowly, let us confess our sins— and then think of God's mercy which can wash the blackest spots on our hearts.

3. The more man turns to God, the more he realises that he is a child of God. God is the King of the universe— the King of all kings. This makes everyone of us a prince, a princess, a son or daughter of the King. If only I remember this one thing that I am the King's son, I will refrain from doing wrong things. I will never stoop low. I will stand up to my royal dignity. I will never compromise with ideals.

4. Avoid occasions: and in that way you will be free from many temptations. It is a good thing for a boy or a man to remove the temptation by removing himself from the occasion.

5. Never forget that impurity begins in the thought. Therefore, take care of your thoughts. Thoughts are forces not to be trifled with: they are the building blocks of life. If you entertain pure thoughts, you build for yourselves a noble future. Otherwise, you work for your own ruination.

6. The moment an evil desire or thought wakes up within you, you should immediately, without the least delay, push it out and punish yourself.

7. An idle mind is the devil's workshop. If you wish to be free from temptations, keep yourself busy all the time.

8. Take care of your food. See that your food is *satvic*, pure, earned by honest means, without doing violence to anyone.

9. Take care of your breathing; breathing has a direct influence upon the mind. Let your breathing be deep and rhythmic.

10. Never succumb to temptation. Try to overcome it but, in spite of your best efforts, if you fail, you must not think any more about it. When a child learns to walk, not unoften, he stumbles and falls. But immediately, the mother comes and lifts him up and asks him to walk again. When you fall, pay no attention to it, but immediately rise and move on— ever onward, forward, Godward!

11. Whenever we are assailed by temptation, let us turn to God.

12. Say to God, "O Lord, I am Thine, completely Thine, utterly Thine! O Lord, I come to Thee as I am. I come to Thee with all my faults and failings, weaknesses and imperfections. Thou wilt shape me, make me, mould me so that Thou art not ashamed of me."

Tension

Do your best then don't worry, be happy.
– Meher Baba

Life today is full of tension. Where may we seek a remedy for it?

It has been said that the natural state of the twentieth century man is tension. Wherever I go, I find people who are tense and nervous. Tension is more common in its incidence than the common cold and certainly it is more harmful and injurious. Thousands of people the world over suffer from hypertension. Today, it seems that we live in an age that is afflicted with tension.

How do we overcome tension? Sri Krishna in the *Gita* gives an answer to this question. Speaking to his dear, devoted disciple Arjuna, the Master says, "O Arjuna! Renouncing all rites and writ duties, come unto Me for single refuge, and I shall liberate you from all bondage to sin and suffering! I shall give you the rest, which your restless heart seeks, of this have no doubt."

In a similar strain did Jesus speak to his people in Jerusalem, "Come unto me, ye that are weary and heavy-laden, and I shall give you rest!"

Do you have a magic mantra by which a person can get rid of his sufferings, pain and tension?

The magic mantra is, *Tum hi sab kuch jaanat priyatam, teri icchha puran ho, sukh mein, dukh mein, mere priyatam, teri icchha puran ho*. The English translation would be, "Thou knowest everything Beloved, let Thy Will always be done! In joy and in sorrow, my Beloved, let Thy Will always be done."

Is there a connection between tension and the pace of life?

Modern life is an unbalanced existence. Everyone is racing for something he does not really want. We are hurrying, hurrying, all the time. Our pace needs to be slowed down. For hurry is the number one cause of tension. And whenever there is tension, we cannot put forth our best efforts. For tension uses up, burns up so much of our energy, which we could utilise in better ways.

It is not only when people are moving that they are in a hurry. Even while they are waiting, mentally they are in a hurry.

Though they may be sitting in an outer office, waiting to be called in for their appointment, or they may be standing, waiting for a friend or a bus, they are in their minds, hurrying. It is this mental hurry that causes tension and keeps on adding to it, until it expresses itself in one physical ailment or another.

Can tension lead to physical illness?

A number of physical illnesses are caused by tension. They range from anxiety, headaches to ulcers. Dr. Guirdham, the author of Cosmic Factors in Disease, has written another book. The title of the book is Obsession. In this book, Dr. Guirdham tells us that tension is the cause of several diseases, including asthma, duodenal ulcers, migraine, malfunctioning of the colon and certain forms of epilepsy. Tension always leads to insomnia or sleeplessness. So it is that the demand for sleeping tablets keeps on growing from day to day. Sleep is a natural, restorative process. After a day's work, a person should be able to sleep peacefully. But, today, in many of our cities, people have lost the ability to sleep.

What is the way of life that we should adopt so that we may not be victims of tension?

The very first suggestion is, adopt a positive attitude towards life. This you cannot do in a day's time. It is a process, but you must start right now.

Secondly, do not anticipate trouble. There are some who

imagine all sorts of troubles— troubles which may never come. Such persons, by anticipating troubles, keep on building up tension.

Thirdly, develop faith! Cultivate faith! What is faith? Faith is not blind. Faith is seeing with the eyes of the heart.

Fourthly, never carry the tension of one moment to another. Has someone harmed you? Has someone spread scandals against you? Has someone behaved rudely towards you? Forget it all, thinking of the unity of all life. You and he are not apart from each other: you and he are but parts of the one whole. In this thought dissolve all tension.

Fifthly, practise relaxation at least twice everyday. There is a yogic *asana*, called *shavasana*, the "dead man's pose". You may learn it from a yogic teacher and as you practise it, you will feel relaxed.

Finally, help others. The others are not apart from us. We and others are parts of the one whole. No man is an island. We must not cut ourselves off from others. If we wish to live a healthy life— mentally, morally, spiritually— we must be concerned about the welfare of others, especially our less fortunate brothers and sisters.

Therapy of Cheerfulness

The best way to cheer yourself up is to cheer somebody else up.
— Mark Twain

It takes 42 muscles to frown; 17 to smile.
— Source Unknown

Cheerfulness is contagious, but don't wait to catch it from others.
Be a carrier!
— Anonymous

Do you believe in the therapy of cheerfulness?

Laughter is a tonic— physical, mental, spiritual. It is a dry cleaner which cleanses you from inside. It gives a new tone to your life. The day on which you have not laughed is a lost day, indeed.

It was Victor Hugo who said, "Laughter is the sun that drives winter from the human face." And George Santayana said, "The young man who has not shed tears is a savage, and the old man who has not laughed is a fool." I would suggest, "The young man who has not shed tears needs to move in the company of the lovers of God and the old man who has not laughed needs the company of the little ones."

Laughter is a medicine. It helps in building up moral muscles. It is a spiritual tonic and has a great cleansing power. When you feel sad or downcast, look at your face in a mirror. It looks so tense, so ugly, so unlike the face you would wish others to see. The strain in the face is due to some negative emotion which is playing havoc in the mind. One way of breaking the force of the negative emotion is to relax. Relax the whole body. And as you do so, you will find that the part of the body to relax last is always the face: and of the face, the mouth is the last part to relax. So smile, and laugh! And you will see how quickly the clouds vanish and you are happy again!

Dada, can cheerfulness improve our health?

Cheerfulness is the new wonder drug. Doctors are of the view that our blood molecules contain receptors which receive signals from the brain. If a person is happy, contented, the receptors transmit these signals of happiness, and the healing process is accelerated. This is a discovery of modern science: as you laugh more, you grow healthier. Jolly physicians, it is said, are better

It diminishes pain, fights disease, mitigates misfortunes, lightens burdens and eases one's life.

Can laughter actually cure diseases?

Today, many doctors are of the view that if a man is happy and light-hearted, cheerful and contented, positive and uncomplaining, disease will not draw close to him and, even if it does, it will not stay with him for long.

Can we keep up the spirit of cheerfulness?

You can and you must. People often ask me which is the most important of the five senses. My reply is always the same: none of them, but the sixth one, the sense of humour. To cultivate it, you must:

1. Get up in the morning with a smile on your face and the words, "Thank you God, for the gift of this new day!" on your lips.

2. See that your face always wears a smile. Rightly said Mahatma Gandhi, "You are not fully dressed until your face wears a smile."

3. Give a hearty laugh at least three times every day—once before breakfast, once before lunch and once before dinner. If you find it difficult to laugh, look into the mirror and make funny faces.

4. Develop a healthy sense of humour. It will save you from many difficult situations.

5. Learn to laugh at yourselves. We often laugh at the oddities and weaknesses of others but not at our own. We must learn to laugh at ourselves.

6. Always look at the bright side of things. Everything has two sides, the bright and the dark or as I would wish to put it, the bright and the less bright.

7. Have faith that God is in charge of the universe. He is the controller of the destiny of individuals and nations and so nothing can ever go wrong.

8. If you would be happy, make others happy. The happiness that goes out of you to others, comes back to you. Such is the law! Therefore, do at least one good deed of service everyday.

"Laughter," says Dr. Wilder, "provides a rhythmic movement of the abdominal muscles, gently massages the intestinal organs, improves digestion and blood circulation."

New prescriptions given by modern physicians are being displayed in hospitals and clinics. "Laugh your way to health"; "Laughter may be hazardous to your illness"; "Cheerfulness is the new wonder drug", are some of them.

What about saints? Are they always serious?

All the great ones of humanity have been lovers of laughter. Socrates, St. Francis of Assisi, St. Teresa of Avilla, Sri Ramakrishna Paramahansa, Sri Ramana Maharishi, Papa Ramdas, Mahatma Gandhi and Sadhu Vaswani, to name but a few, all possessed a deep sense of humour.

Mahatma Gandhi said, "If I didn't have a sense of humour, I would have committed suicide long ago."

Papa Ramdas said, "I did not have to shed tears. I laughed my way to God."

Sadhu Vaswani had a sparkling wit and humour, which would make us, at times, burst with laughter. One day, a doctor came to him and said, "I have decided to give up my practice, and devote all my time to the service of the country."

Sadhu Vaswani said to us, "I am not sure if he has given up his practice or his practice has given him up!"

Does God laugh ?

Yes, God does laugh! He never laughs at our weaknesses and imperfections, our heartaches and headaches. But He does laugh at the ungodly world which thinks it can efface God out of existence.

He laughs at our schools and colleges where, in the name of secularism, a Godless education is given to our boys and girls, the "builders of tomorrow".

God laughs when some of us remark that we can teach God how to make a better world. There is a wealthy woman who rejoices in saying, "I wish God made me His secretary, I would teach Him how to make a better and happier world!"

I believe it was Sri Ramakrishna Paramahansa who said, "God laughs when a doctor assures his patient that if he takes his medicine, he will recover soon. God laughs, for He knows that the man is going to die that very night."

God laughs also, when two brothers get together and say, this property is mine and that is yours. God laughs, for He knows that all properties belong to mother earth.

Thought -Power

*All that we are is the result of what we have thought. It is founded on
our thoughts and made up of our thoughts.*
– Dhammapada

Thoughts are the ink in the pen with which we are writing our destiny.
–J. P. V.

Dada, it is said that as you think so you become. Is this true?

Yes— this is what the *rishis* of ancient India taught thousands of years ago. I am happy this truth has been reaffirmed, in our days, by some of the Western thinkers, scientists and industrialists. When the question was asked of Benjamin Franklin, "What is the greatest discovery of our generation?" he answered, "The greatest discovery of our generation is that by changing one's thought pattern, one can change one's life." As you think so you become.

Often times, we pay scant attention to our thoughts. We say, after all it was but a thought. We must never forget that thoughts are things, thoughts are forces, thoughts are the building blocks of life. With thoughts, we are building the edifice of our own life, building our own future. People blame their stars, their destiny. "Men heap together the mistakes of their lives," said John Oliver Hobbes, "and create a monster they call destiny." Destiny is not a matter of chance; it is a matter of choice. We are building our own destiny everyday, with the thoughts that we think. A thought, if it is constantly held in the mind, will drive us to action. If it is a thought of service, it will lead us to an act of service. If it is a thought of impurity, it will lead us to an act of impurity.

An action, which is repeated, creates a habit. And a habit is a terrible thing. Take away its "h", and "a bit" will remain. Take away the "a" and "bit" will still remain. Take away "b" and "it" will still remain.

The sum total of our habits forms our character. It is character that determines our destiny. If we wish to change our destiny, we must begin with the thought. We must change our pattern of thinking. We must cleanse the mind of all the dirt which we have accumulated through the years. Our minds need to be cleansed of thoughts of lust, hatred and greed, passion and pride, selfishness and miserliness, avarice and arrogance, envy and jealousy, resentment and ill-will.

There are those who nurture thoughts of hatred, envy and jealousy in their hearts. How can they ever hope to be happy? Hatred and happiness can never dwell together, even as darkness and light can never live together. There was a man who met me a long time ago. He said, "There is a fire burning within my heart: it will not be quenched until I have shot down the man who was indirectly responsible for the death of my father." How true! Hatred is a fire which keeps burning within the heart: it burns away all your happiness.

Do thoughts have a form?

Every thought survives and has a form and colour. A thought may have the form of an angel or a demon depending upon its contents. If I think a thought of peace, purity, prayer, love, joy, sympathy or service, it will stick to me wearing the form of an angel. If I think a thought of envy, jealousy, hatred, ill-will, resentment, greed or dishonesty, it will stick to me wearing the form of a demon.

Each one of us has around him these forms— angelic or demoniac— depending upon the type of thoughts he thinks.

These forms draw to themselves forms of a like nature. If we are surrounded by demoniac forms, they attract to themselves many more demons.

We have heard of physically weak people performing heroic deeds of valour far beyond their physical strength. From where do they get all that strength? The seemingly impossible is accomplished when determination is accompanied by high purpose. Referring to Sir Galahad, Tennyson says, "His strength was the strength of ten, because his heart was pure!"

Low thoughts have an evil and disturbing effect. Sometimes, in a fit of temper, we do things of which we are otherwise not capable. Later, as we repent for evil deeds, we exclaim, "Some devil must have tempted me!" We are not attacked by these entities: we attract them to ourselves.

How do thoughts affect our lives?

There are so many people, who through their thoughts, draw to themselves calamities and misfortunes. Doctors, today, speak of a new disease. They call it "symptomatic imaginities". A person has simple symptoms and he begins to imagine that he has contracted a dreaded disease. There is a woman, who, if she gets a headache, begins to imagine that she has developed a tumour in the brain. There is a man who, whenever he gets a stomach ache feels he has developed cancer of the stomach. By imagining and thinking thus, we draw those diseases to ourselves. Therefore, we must be very careful about our thoughts.

Are we creators of our own destiny?

We are the architects of our own destiny. We are the builders of our own fate. Many of us blame fate, *kismet* for our misfortune. But let me tell you, dear friends, that you are the builders of your own fate. Therefore, be careful, especially of your thoughts. We pay scant attention to our thoughts, believing that they are of no consequence. We say, after all, it was only a thought, what does it matter? Every thought is a seed you are sowing in the field of life, and what you sow today, you will have to reap tomorrow.

God has created a universe of beauty, fullness, happiness and harmony. Each one of us is a child of God. God wishes each one of us to be happy, healthy, prosperous, successful and to enjoy all the good things He has created. We keep ourselves away from all those bounties because of our *karma*. Change your *karma* and you will change the conditions in which you live. You can change your *karma* by adopting a new pattern of thinking.

Can you give us some suggestions on thought control?

So many of our ills would be cured, if only we could change the pattern of our mind. Change the mind, and you change the world. The modern world has gone astray, because it lays undue emphasis on the "work" side of life. Work has its place in life, but more important than "work" is "thought". Take care of your thoughts. Every thought is a force which we generate for our good or evil.

Some may well remark, thoughts come to us from God knows where. They overwhelm us; and we feel helpless. Is it our fault that evil thoughts come to us, from time to time?

No, it is not our fault if evil thoughts come to us and tear into bits the fabric of a good life which we may have gradually built. But it is our fault if we welcome evil thoughts and let them germinate in the soil of our minds. Out of them will grow trees of bitter fruits which we shall be compelled to swallow.

Behind every evil thought is an evil force. When we accept evil thoughts, we, as it were, attach ourselves to dark powers. We fall into their clutches, and before we know it, we create "hell" for ourselves.

If we think good thoughts— thoughts of love and compassion, beauty and joy, faith and freedom, of peace and wisdom— we invite to ourselves good forces, forces of light and, in that measure, we create heaven around ourselves.

Some suggestions that you may find useful are as follows:

1. Perhaps, the simplest and most efficacious method of correcting our thinking is that of *kirtan*. Whenever two or three gather together, let them sing in chorus, the Name Divine, and in the Name lose themselves, drown themselves. This method is so simple that often its importance is overlooked. But it is one of immense value to us all.

Are our homes breaking? Is our community crumbling? Are nations at war with each other? The cure of these and other ills is *kirtan*. O ye pilgrims on the path! Get together and form *kirtan*-bands. You will sanctify your own lives. You will purify— as did Sri Chaitanya centuries ago— the atmosphere of your town and country: you will release forces for the healing of the human race.

2. As you wake up in the morning, breathe out an aspiration of purity, love, joy, peace, humility, trust— any aspiration that may express your innermost need. Repeat this aspiration as often as you can during the day, even in the midst of your work.

3. As you retire at night, read a little from the life or teaching of a saint, a *bhakta*, a man of God. This has a purifying influence on the mind and, consequently, on one's dream-consciousness.

4. When evil thoughts come to you, do not struggle with them. The more you struggle, the more you strengthen them. The best way to face evil thoughts is to let them alone and to think divine thoughts. Light dispels darkness. Every good

5. Keep yourself relaxed at all times, both in body and mind. So, work with moderate speed: and speak gently, sweetly, in love and understanding. Let nothing disturb your inner peace. Imagine the world as an ocean in which stormy waves rise high, threatening to drown you. Be still and full of trust in the Lord of the Ocean. The waves will pass away. In all difficulties and dangers, believe with the ancient seer who exclaimed, "All is well, a thousand times well, both now and a million years hence!"

Is it true that we are our own enemies?

The *Bhagavad Gita* says, "Man is his own friend: man is his own foe!" We are our own friends and we are our own enemies. No one outside of us can do us any harm. It is very easy, in difficult and trying circumstances, to throw the blame on others. It is very easy to say that if such and such a thing had not occurred, our condition would have been different. That is not so! No one outside of us can do us harm. It is we who are our own foes, we who can be our own friends. If we would be our own friends, let us adopt a positive attitude towards life. The positive attitude is the friendly attitude.

What is positive thinking?

It is not that the man with a positive attitude refuses to recognise the negative side of life. Life has a negative side, a dark side. The pathways of life are strewn with difficulties. But the man with the positive attitude refuses to dwell on the negative side of life. He looks for the best results from the worst conditions. Surrounded by trials and tribulations, he looks for some place to

Conditions may be adverse, yet he continues to expect good things. It is an inviolable law of life, that when you expect good, good will come to you.

There are people who are always thinking negative. Speak to them about something, and they will tell you, "It can't be done! It is impossible!" There are people who always think in terms of disease and death. Those are the ones who, through the magnetic power of their own thoughts, draw disease to themselves. They are their own enemies.

The man with the friendly attitude will always count his blessings. He may find himself in very deep waters, yet he will look around for something for which he may feel grateful.

Understanding

Grant that we may not so much seek to be understood as to understand.
— St. Francis of Assisi

ration Life D...
Egoism, Violent Dreams *Spirituality*
Seeker Service Silence Spirituality
Vibrations Willpower Woman Yoga...
Of The World Bhagvad Gita God...
Selfishness Frustration, Worry...
Rituals Sadhu Vaswani Science An...
Thought Power Understanding Vega
Education Faith Fear For...
Meditation M...
And I...

Dada, why do misunderstandings occur?

The word "understand" says to us, "stand under". No one is prepared today, to stand under anyone. Everybody wants to stand over everybody. That is the main cause of misunderstanding.

No two people seem to understand each other today. Why is this so?

The greatest famine in the world, today, is the famine of understanding. It is true no two people seem to be able to understand one another. That is why we hear those words, "Why don't you understand me?" The age we live in is an age in which misunderstandings abound— misunderstandings in our homes, our clubs, our schools, colleges, universities, our temples and churches.

I recall the words of the great Parsi prophet, Zoroaster, "Know well that a hundred temples of wood and stone have not the value of one single understanding heart!" Understanding hearts are needed.

King Solomon prayed, "Lord! Thou hast granted me so many things. Grant me one thing more. Grant me an understanding heart."

Give us a few tips to help us cultivate the spirit of understanding.

If you wish to grow in the spirit of understanding you must:

1. Learn to be a good listener— let the other person talk and express his point of view.

2. Do not belittle the other person, do not make him feel small. Do not criticise him or find fault with him.

3. When you find you cannot get along well with others, do

Liberation Life
Egoism Violent Dream
Seeker Service Silence Spirituality
Vibrations Willpower Woman Yoga
Of The World Bhagavad Gita
Selfishness Frustration Worry
Rituals Sadhu Vaswani Science
Thought Power Understanding
Education Faith Fear
Meditation

not blame them; find the fault in yourself.

4   Remember there can be no true understanding without the spirit of humility.

5   Avoid arguments: when you think you have won an argument, you may have actually lost a friend.

6   Even when you don't agree with people, respect their opinion.

7   Always be on the lookout for opportunities to be of service to others; learn to be sensitive to others' needs.

Vegetarianism

Of a certainty the man who can see all creatures in himself, himself in all creatures, knows no sorrow
— Isa Upanishad

Preventing pain to an animal is a command of the Torah.
— Mishnah, Shabbath, 128

"Hurt not the animal", said he, "for within it is the soul of your own sister."
— George Burrow, The Bible in Spain (1834)

To become vegetarian is to step into the stream which leads to nirvana.
— Gautama Buddha

here is no beast on earth, no bird which flieth but ... the same is a people like unto you. All God's creatures are God's family.
— The Holy Quran

Do you think vegetarianism as a concept will be acceptable to the world at large?

There was a time when vegetarianism was tolerated as a "cult of the crazy". It became the butt of many jokes. One of them concerned a man who suffered from insomnia, sleeplessness. The doctor advised him to induce sleep by counting sheep.

The man answered, "I can't do that because I am a vegetarian."

The doctor said, "Then count carrots."

Today the tide has turned. An ever increasing number of people all over the world are turning to vegetarianism as a way of life which leads to health and strength of the body, mind and soul.

Will a vegetarian diet give me all the nutrition that I need?

A number of people are under the impression that they and their children cannot be strong unless they eat food of violence. Meat gives strength to the body, they say. Without meat, the body becomes weak and a prey to many diseases.

As an answer to this query, the example is given of the elephant which is one of the biggest and strongest animals in the world: and the elephant is a pure vegetarian.

"What of the lion?" someone will ask. The elephant cannot match his strength against that of the lion. True, but the lion has destructive strength, while the elephant has the strength that can be used in the service of humanity. The elephant carries huge logs of wood from one place to another. Can you make a lion do likewise? Perhaps yes, but at the risk of your own life. It was Shakespeare who said, "O, it is excellent to have a giant's strength, but it is tyrannous to use it like a giant."

ration Violence
Seeker Service Silence of
Vibrations Willpower Woman Bhagavan
Of The World Selfishness Frustration
Rituals Sadhu Vaswani
Thought Power Understanding
Education Faith Fear For
Meditation M
And

Isn't a vegetarian diet low in protein?

It is commonly believed that you cannot get sufficient protein from a vegetarian diet. Meat, it is said, is the only source of protein. At a question-answer session, where I referred to the advantages of a low-fat, vegetarian diet, a man got up and objected that no one gets enough protein without eating meat.

When I asked him what protein was, he fumbled and answered, "I do not know what protein is but I know that everyone needs it."

"How much protein does a man need?" I asked him.

"I cannot tell you exactly", was his answer, "but we need lots and lots of protein to keep the body alive."

Many of us, I am afraid, are unaware of the real needs of the body. Protein is something that you have in every living thing, vegetable and animal. It is very plentiful. Next to water, it is the most plentiful substance in the body. Its function is to help build muscles, blood, skin, hair, nails, and all the organs of the body.

How much protein does a person need to take in everyday?

It varies from individual to individual. It depends upon a person's weight, sex and the type of work he does. The quantity of protein that a person needs is not much. In fact, if you take more protein than what is required it may lead to degenerative diseases such as osteoporosis and obesity. If you are twenty years or over, the total quantity of protein that you need per day (in gms.) can be estimated by multiplying your weight (in pounds) by 0.36. For instance, if you are 25 years of age and you weigh 110 pounds, your daily protein requirement is 110 x 0.36 = 39.6gms or say 40 gms. An average minimum protein requirement is around 45 gms a day. All the protein you need is easily available in milk (preferably skimmed, to remove the excessive fat), curds, and cheese, lentils, soyabeans, peanuts, and sunflower seeds. You do not have to worry about your protein. The world famous nutritionist, Earl Mindell, writes in the Vitamin Bible, "A good rice and beans dish, with some cheese can be as nourishing, less expensive, and lower in fat than a steak."

In point of quality, the protein that is present in vegetarian food is superior to that obtained from meat diet. Dr. Christopher Gian Cuisio, a nutritionist of repute, tells us that vegetables "are primary sources nourished by the sun and soil while meat is a secondary source nourished and sustained by vegetables." Most of the animals killed for food, live on a vegetarian diet. Why then, must we not go to the source of nutrition, viz. vegetarian food?

If it is cruel to kill animals, how is it that some of the great world religions have sanctioned meat eating? Even Jesus, one of the most compassionate of men, ate meat!

There is growing evidence pointing to the fact that Jesus and his immediate followers abstained from food of violence and were all vegetarians. The version that we have of Jesus is the one given in the New Testament. There are several versions of Jesus, not as popular, but worth considering. The New Testament was written years after the Crucifixion of Jesus and by those who had not come in personal contact with him. The most ancient gospel in existence is the Gospel, according to the Ebionities. It tells us that Jesus and John the Baptist were vegetarians. Also James, the Just, who was close to Jesus was a staunch vegetarian. The early church historian, Hegesippus, writing about 160 AD., says that James "drank no wine, nor strong drink, nor ate animal food."

The Essene Gospel of Peace tells us that one day the disciples asked Jesus, "What are the sins we must shun, that we may never more see disease? " And Jesus answered, "It was said to them of old time, 'Honor thy Heavenly Father and thy earthly Mother and do their commandments, that their days may be long upon the earth." And next afterwards, "Which God has given, let not man take away. For I tell you truly, he who kills himself, and he who eats the flesh of slain beasts, eats the body of death."

It is for scholars to determine which version (of Jesus) is the correct one. I love to think of Jesus as a master of compassion and mercy.

Has not God created birds and beasts, fish and fowl to fulfill man's needs?

The ancient *rishi* of the *Ishopanishad* sang, "*Ishavasyam idam sarvam.*" "All that is, is a vesture of the Lord!" God comes to us, putting on different vestures, different garments. Clad in different garbs, the Lord comes to us to test us, to find out if we truly love Him, as we say we do. Alas, we slay the Lord! We handle Him roughly, we treat Him harshly. We offer Him worship in temples and churches. We chant hymns to His glory, but out in the street we are cruel to Him. We slay Him and eat His flesh. We forget that the animal, too, is an image of God!

Much on earth is masked. But there is a strange, a mystic sense of fellowship with all that lives. This is what makes every life sacred.

Dada, they say it is wrong to eat meat, but then if our husbands and children eat, isn't it our duty to cook for them?

Yes, it is. You must do your duty. You must be true to yourself but you need not eat meat. There was a saint in Sind. Sadna was his name. He was a butcher, yet, he rose to the level of sainthood. Therefore, you have to do your duty.

For a student of biology, is dissection wrong?

It is a question that each one of you will have to decide for yourself. It is meaningless to have so much dissection in the college and university laboratories. That very work could be done by studying a model of a frog. It is not necessary to give pain to a frog.

Perhaps, there was a time when it was felt necessary to dissect a frog for gaining medical knowledge. It is no longer necessary today. It is meaningless. Man has yet to understand that there is only one life, that the same life that is in him, is also in the frog. I think the time has come when the students should think of this matter and say, why kill when it is not necessary? You get such wonderful models of frogs. You can study them. They are doing it now in the West— in England and in America. There are a number of anti-vivesection societies. They have taken up this matter in hand.

What is your opinion of vivisection—experimenting on animals for scientific advancement?

Knowledge is not knowledge which is acquired in cruel ways. Such ill-gotten knowledge is a curse: it unleashes the very forces of hell and will hurl humanity into a dark abyss of disease and death. Knowledge, if it is to be a source of blessing to humanity, must never be sought through the torturing of helpless creatures. True knowledge springs from compassion and love.

If the world turns vegetarian, the global biological system will get upset. This might eventually lead to our own death. When the

world is going to turn vegetarian, how are we going to overcome this problem?

Firstly, you must not bother about so many things. It is not your domain. If you were put in charge, if you were *Brahma*, the Creator of the universe, then of course it is your duty. But not otherwise. You must not poke your nose, as they say, in a domain which does not belong to you.

Secondly, due to breeding, the population of animals is growing today. If the population grew in a natural way there would be no problem at all. No bio-problem will occur. Nature knows how to take care of its own creation.

We use artificial methods for breeding animals to make money. It is not merely breeding animals, but do you know that cows are given Stilbestrol injections when they are in pregnancy so that they put on more flesh? So that when they are slaughtered it brings more money to the owner of the cow? You do not know how many millions of animals are born through this process of breeding. If only you could do away with the artificial methods there would be no bio-problem at all. Nature will know how to take care of it.

This talk about over population has no sense, because nature will provide. But if we take the law of nature in our own hands, then the responsibility devolves on us.

Why do you observe November 25 as an 'International Meatless Day'?

Sadhu Vaswani was a voice of the voiceless ones, the dumb, the defenceless children of God who, alas are being slain by the millions in our soulless cities everyday. "O, the sin of daily slaughter!" he exclaimed. And he added words with which many today will not be in sympathy. But he spoke with the foresight of a seer when he said, "Believe me, the day is coming when meat-eating will be condemned as murder!" He also said, "I have seen God's image shining in birds and animals, and for me not to love bird and animal would be not to love the Lord!" It was therefore felt appropriate, that the 25th of November, the birthday of this humble, holy man of God, this prophet of reverence for all life, be observed, year after year, as an 'International Meatless Day and Animal Rights' Day'. The suggestion came from one of Sadhu Vaswani's devotees who lives in the United States of America. The suggestion was taken by the Sadhu Vaswani Mission and centres all over India in different countries of the world. And you will be happy to know that the response we have received so far is very encouraging.

But, Dada, why just one day?

Just one day, because the idea is to create an awareness in the minds of the people in regard to the cruelties that are perpetrated on animals and birds day after day. When a delicious dish is placed before a man, he eats it as a matter of course. He does not realise, he never thinks of the agony through which the slaughtered animal must have passed.

Do you know that on an average a human being eats 7,500 big and small animals during a lifetime? 7,500 animals, every one of whom loves life as well as do those who eat them up. The time has come when we must recognise the moral inviolability of the individual, whether human or non-human.

Even as the black people do not exist as resources for the whites, even as women do not exist as resources for men, even so animals do not exist as resources for human beings. The time is come when animals should be given, must be given, certain fundamental rights.

They say that we must not kill animals, as they feel pain. But surely, plants too, have life. How can we eat them? It seems as if whatever we eat, we are causing pain. Should we then starve to death as soon as we are born?

The human birth has been given us for a specific purpose. Until that purpose is fulfilled, we must continue to live. This should be done by causing the least pain to other forms of life. When we pluck a vegetable, the pain caused to it is infinitesimally small as compared to the pain caused to an animal when it is slaughtered. Animals like human beings, are five-sensed creatures and feel the pain as much as we do.

Further, there are different degrees of sensitivity to pain. Plants cannot feel as much pain as animals do when they are killed because as was pointed out by Sir Jagdish Chandra Bose, plants have not developed a nervous system. Living on this earth-plane, we have to sustain our life. But our ideal must be to commit the least violence, cause the least pain to others. This we do, when we live on vegetables instead of on animal flesh.

Dr. Albert Schweitzer, the great prophet of reverence for life, gave us this beautiful example. There is a man who is carrying a bundle of grass to feed his cattle. He has mowed the grass, cut it and bundled it, but in so doing, he has committed no wrong, because the grass is needed to keep his cattle alive. But as he walks on the roadside, he plucks a leaf from a tree— this, according to Dr. Schweitzer, is a wanton act of violence: it is needless, and therefore wrong. The leaf is not required to support any form of life, and it is needless to cause pain to it by plucking it.

What can we do to avoid eating food of violence, when one is born in a meat-eating family?

That is entirely upto the individual! But there have been many people who were born in meat-eating families, who turned away from flesh-food when their hearts awoke to become sensitive to the pain of other creatures.

Sadhu Vaswani was born in a family of *Kali* worshippers. They regarded meat as *prasad*, and it was even distributed in the temple. One day, when he was barely six or seven years old, he happened to pass by a butcher's shop and saw pieces of flesh hanging there. When he enquired what those things were, his friends laughed at him and told him, "That is what you eat, day after day." "Where does it come from?" he wanted to know; and they told him, "This is what you get by slaughtering animals." He was shocked! "Have I been eating this food of violence all these years?" he asked himself. "I shall do it no longer." He returned home and told his mother that he would rather starve than eat meat henceforth.

Soon thereafter, his father took him to the temple. It was a sacred day and the priest was distributing meat as *prasad*. When it was offered to Sadhu Vaswani, the child refused to touch it! "How can you refuse *prasad*?" said the angry father. And Sadhu Vaswani replied, "You say that Kali is the Mother of the universe. How can She be happy if you kill one of Her children and offer its meat as *prasad*?"

Nobody could answer his question. The father was very annoyed and told his son, "I will never bring you to the temple, ever again." "I have already decided never to enter a temple where meat is distributed as *prasad*!" exclaimed the child.

You may be born in a meat-eating family, or in a country where flesh food is a rule, rather than an exception. But it is up to you to decide what is right for you.

Dear Dada, what can we do to show to the world what an offence killing helpless animals is?

The *tapasya* of the tongue is very difficult. People are slaves to the tongue. But we can influence the world, only through our own example. Gradually the influence will keep on growing. It is like throwing a pebble in a pool of water. When a pebble is thrown it creates ripples. Likewise, the influence of a person who bears witness to an ideal in his daily life, creates ripples of influence.

Dada, you just referred to the tapasya of the tongue. Can you elucidate?

The *tapasya* of the tongue has two aspects.

1. Control of taste.

2. Control of speech.

Just to get a momentary pleasure of taste, people slay innocent creatures everyday and devour their flesh. Even though meat-eating has been proved injurious to health, to satisfy their palate, men become slaves to the tongue. The second aspect is the control over speech.

They who know, tell us, that life can never be killed. It is the forms which perish. Why then must we feel sad if birds and animals are slaughtered?

Life, it is true, is eternal. It is also true that the law of life is compassion and love. Out of love cometh joy and every other blessing. He who hath not experienced love hath not known what it is to love.

All killing is a denial of love. For to kill or to eat what another has killed, is to rejoice in cruelty. And cruelty hardens our heart and blinds our vision and we see not that they whom we kill are our brothers and sisters in the one brotherhood of life.

He who kills another, kills himself. He who feeds on death himself becomes food for death. He who inflicts suffering upon another, brings suffering to himself. Such is the law!

Every bit of flesh you tear, you will be called upon to repair with your own flesh! Every limb you mutilate, you will be compelled to replace with your own limb. And every bone you break, you will be asked to mend with your own bone!

Dada, what are the marks of a true vegetarian?

The true vegetarian, as I think of him, is filled through and through with reverence for life. He reveres life as a gift of God which no man can bestow and, therefore, will not destroy. Such a one has the following marks:

1. His heart is a flowing river of compassion and love. The basis of true compassion is a feeling of unity, of oneness with all creatures that breathe the breath of life. I, and that tiny winged creature that hovers round yon lamp, are one. Men and animals and birds, fish and fowl, moths and mosquitoes— all, all are one— in the One without whom there is no other.

To the true vegetarian, therefore, each life-unit is as dear and precious as his own life. To him every dumb creature of God is his own self wearing another body. And so the true vegetarian will be no party to any movement for slaughter. On his banner are inscribed the words in letters of fire: Stop all slaughter!

2. The true vegetarian is a man of self-discipline. So many there are who do not eat flesh but, alas, they easily succumb to the flesh. They cannot resist the temptations of the flesh. They are soft: they have not put out the fire of passion. The true vegetarian is unswayed by passion, unruffled by anger, unmoved by greed and gold.

3. The true vegetarian is a man of humility. Deep in his heart he knows that he is not free from the sin of killing. For to breathe is to kill the germs that are in the air around us. To talk is to kill; to walk is to kill. Indeed, to live is to kill.

4. Living in such a world, the true vegetarian becomes a worshipper, a man of prayer. He sees cruelty all around him. How many hearts can he touch? How many lives can he save? And so he turns to Him who is the one Saviour of all. The true vegetarian prays alike for the killer and the killed and he prays that he may become an instrument of God's love in this world of anguish and pain.

5. The true vegetarian is a man of indomitable faith. He believes profoundly that life is entirely a gift of God. In periods of crisis, in times of famine and flood, his mind wavers not! He prefers starvation to eating impure food.

To the Sufi *dervish*, Abu Ala Maeera, his physician said, "O man of God! Why will you not live longer and bless this earth? Drink this chicken soup I have brought you and see how quickly health and strength returns to your feeble body." The *dervish* laughed heartily and said, "Must you offer me the soup of a weak, defenceless creature who cannot strike back in return? It is not worthy of you! Bring me the soup of a lion's cub!"

Do you think flesh-diet slows down our spiritual progress?

As far as spiritual progress is concerned, the teaching that has come down to us from the *Gita* is that we must eat *satvic* food, as far as possible. Food of violence— flesh, fish, fowl— is not *satvic* food. I must admit, however, that there are non-vegetarians who are highly spiritual. But, in general, I would say, it is always helpful to take *satvic* food. Even cooked food (vegetarian) should be taken in moderation and uncooked food, like salads and fruits should be taken in plenty.

Vibrations

*Use what talent you possess. The woods would be very silent
if no birds sang there except those that sang best.*
— *Rev. Oliver Wilson*

Dada, sometimes we take an instant dislike to a person we meet. Why is it so?

There is the law of vibrations. Each one of us is vibrating to a particular frequency. Have you done physics? You must have seen those tuning forks. They vibrate to 118, 186, 212 and so on. Each one of us is just like a tuning fork. We are all vibrating to a particular frequency. The frequency at which you are vibrating is not the frequency at which I am vibrating.

When our vibrations are in harmony with each other, we like each other. But if they are in disharmony, then for no apparent reason, we get a feeling of dislike. We don't like to draw close to that person, because of our vibrations.

How can we increase the rate of our vibrations?

The way to increase the rate of vibrations is to be less physical and more ethereal, less physical and more spiritual. The Spirit is vibratory. In the measure in which I invite the Spirit into my life, in that measure I will be more and more vibratory. There are so many who are *sthula*, just physical. Their lives are those of animals. concerning them the Great Guru said, "*Kartut pashu key manish jaat.*" They appear to be like humans but their actions are like those of animals.

Are vibrations powerful?

Every vibration, as you know, contains a certain power. There are vibrations that are very powerful, while others are less powerful. Each one of us is a generator of vibrations. There are people with such powerful vibrations that they can move out and heal other people. They can move out and help other people.

Therefore, we go to holy ones and we tell them to pray for us, to bless us. The vibrations of holy ones generate tremendous power.

Dadaji, what is a blessing?

A blessing is a vibration that moves out of the holy ones to us. Sadhu Vaswani used to say that saints are more vibratory than vocal. They may not speak a single word but strong vibrations emanate from them. They come and touch our hearts. They come and affect our lives without having to speak a single word.

Will Power

Will power is being able to eat just one salted peanut.
— Pat Elphinstone

Will power should be understood to be the strength of mind which makes
it capable of meeting success or failure with equanimity.
— Ramana Maharishi

ation Life Violent Dream Silence Spiritual Yoga
geism Service Silence Spiritual Yoga Woman Yoga Worry Science
Seeker Vibrations Willpower Of The World Bhagavad Gita Thought-Power Understanding
Selfishness Rituals Sadhu Sadhu Vaswani Science
Frustration Thought-Power Education Faith Fear Forg
Meditation Mi And C

Dadaji, why is it so difficult to develop will power?

In the *Upanishads*, the *rishi* says that there are two paths open to each one of us at every step in life. One path he calls *preya*; the other, *shreya*. *Preya* is the pleasant way. It is a smooth and slippery path. *Shreya* is the good, the perfect; but the pathway is rugged and steep.

It is always easier to move along the smooth and slippery road, than to climb a steep and rugged path. To climb the rugged path you need will power. And for will power you must pray again and again and still again. Will power will come to you as a gift from God. In the *Bhagavad Gita*, Lord Krishna refers to the tortoise. He says that once the tortoise draws in its limbs, even if you cut it into four pieces, you will not be able to take out its limbs. Such will power must be developed. But this comes through practice and through control over one's thoughts. Our minds must be filled with the thought of God if we are to grow in will power, otherwise it is very easy to slip.

Gautama Buddha observes that the temptations, *vikaras*, passions come to man even as rain comes in through a tiny hole in the roof of a cottage. Rain finds its way through such holes. Even if there is only one tiny hole in it, water will find its way. Likewise with passion; it will find its way even if there is a tiny hole in your mind.

Dada, how should we differentiate between control and suppression? If a feeling or an emotion is suppressed it is bound to bounce back. So how should we differentiate?

We must not suppress anything but we should sublimate it, refer it to the Lord. Supposing a temptation comes to you, you must not resist it. If you suppress it, it is likely to create complexes in your subconscious mind. But refer it to the Lord.

Dada, can you suggest some simple disciplines to increase our will power.

Firstly, through repeated prayer. "Ask and it shall be given unto thee," said Jesus.

Secondly, by resolving to keep away from something which you relish. For example, if you are very fond of sweets, try and give up eating sweets for a week. If you are addicted to watching movies, avoid movies for a few weeks. This will strengthen your will power.

And thirdly, you can strengthen your will power through studies of biographies and sayings of men and women of will power.

Woman

The woman-soul has the shakti to rebuild the shattered world
in the strength of her intuitions, her purity, her simplicity,
her spiritual aspirations, her sympathy and silent sacrifice.
The woman-soul will lead us upward, on!
— Sadhu Vaswani

Dada, why is woman given such importance in our culture?

Woman is the transmitter of tradition from one generation to another. Woman is the builder of the home which is one of the two centres where character is built— the other one being the school. When the child's mind is still plastic, the mother can influence it to grow in the right direction. The mother can sow seeds of character and idealism in the receptive mind of the child. When the child becomes a teenager, he comes under other influences. It has been rightly said that if you educate a boy, you but educate an individual, whereas if you educate a girl, you educate an entire family.

Significant are the words of Theodore Roosevelt, "The mother is the one supreme asset of national life. She is more important, by far, than a successful statesman, or businessman, or artist or scientist."

Sadhu Vaswani, the founder of the Mira Movement in Education, often said, "The woman-soul will lead us upward on!" Can you elaborate on it?

The man-made world is already crumbling beneath the burden of its own weight. For man has bungled and greatly blundered. Man has believed in physical force— in the atom bomb, nuclear weapons, star-wars. A new world is in the making. Of this new world, the builder will not be man, but woman— the true woman, the authentic woman, who will be true to her own purpose and being. The French author and politician, Joseph Marie de Maistre, said, "The great fault in women is their desire to be like men."

Woman is the symbol of *shakti. Shakti*, not physical force, but integration. The woman-soul will rebuild the shattered world in her *shakti*, the strength of her intuitions, her purity and faith in prayer, her simplicity and sympathy and service, her spiritual aspiration and silent sacrifice.

Yoga

The highest Yoga is the control of the mind.
– Srimad Bhagavatam

Can you ever see God if you do not direct your whole mind toward Him?
The Bhagavata speaks about Sukadeva. When he walked about he looked
like a soldier with fixed bayonet. His gaze did not wander: it had only one
goal and that was God. This is the meaning of Yoga.
– Sri Ramakrishna Paramahansa

What is yoga?

The word, "*yoga*", is derived from the Sanskrit word *yug* which means "to unite". *Yoga* is the science of union. We live in a world of separateness from the Divine Source whom, for want of a better word, we call God. God is the source of true happiness. He is the source of everything that is good, true and beautiful. As long as we live in separation from God, so long shall we continue to be unhappy. The way to God is the way of *yoga*.

What is the purpose of yoga?

The literal meaning of the word "*yoga*" is "union". Union with what? Union with whom? We live in a world of separateness, and so are unhappy. We need a unifying vision of life.

We come from a divine source. After coming here, we have built up an artificial world, a world of separateness, and so are unhappy. We cannot be happy until we re-unite with the Divine.

How do we re-unite with the Divine? To do my duty and, in the midst of difficulties and danger, to have peace within me– is the way of yoga. Storms may blow around me— yet I retain inner peace, the rest of the soul.

Yoga is not running away from the world to the peak of a holy hill or to a forest of meditation. Yoga is to be in the world but not of the world. Yoga is to stay in the world but not let worldliness stay within you.

How may this be done, Dada?

By entering into the depths within. The emphasis, today, is on widening the surface. Yoga teaches us to plumb the depths of life.

What is the way to do this, Dada?

The answer is in a few simple words. Learn to concentrate and develop meditation. Meditation will take you deeper and deeper within yourself and, one day, you will know who you really are.

Do we have to renounce the world in order to take up yoga?

To do my duty, in the midst of all difficulties, to have peace within me— that is the way of *yoga*. *Yoga* is not running away from life. *Yoga* is to live in the world and not be of the world. *Yoga* is the conquest of circumstances and environment.

Dada which is the easiest yoga?

It is *sahaja yoga*— the simple *yoga*. To practise it you must:

1. Develop fellowship with a living *yogi*.

2. Cultivate love of silence.

3. Never neglect your daily appointment with God.

4. Kill all desires for personal popularity.

5. Offer all your work to the Lord.

6. Help others, beholding in them images of the Eternal.

Is yoga meant for the common man?

Yoga is not the monopoly of a chosen few. *Yoga* is open to everyone. It is open to you and to me. For *yoga*, cumbersome or difficult breathing exercises are not necessary. When Sadhu Vaswani was asked, "Do you practise *pranayama*? he answered, "My *pranayama* is *Rama Nama*!" He was a *yogi*, a true friend of God. Go out in quest of such a one. Having found him, surrender yourself to him completely. He will lead you ever onward, forward, upward, inward, and Godward!